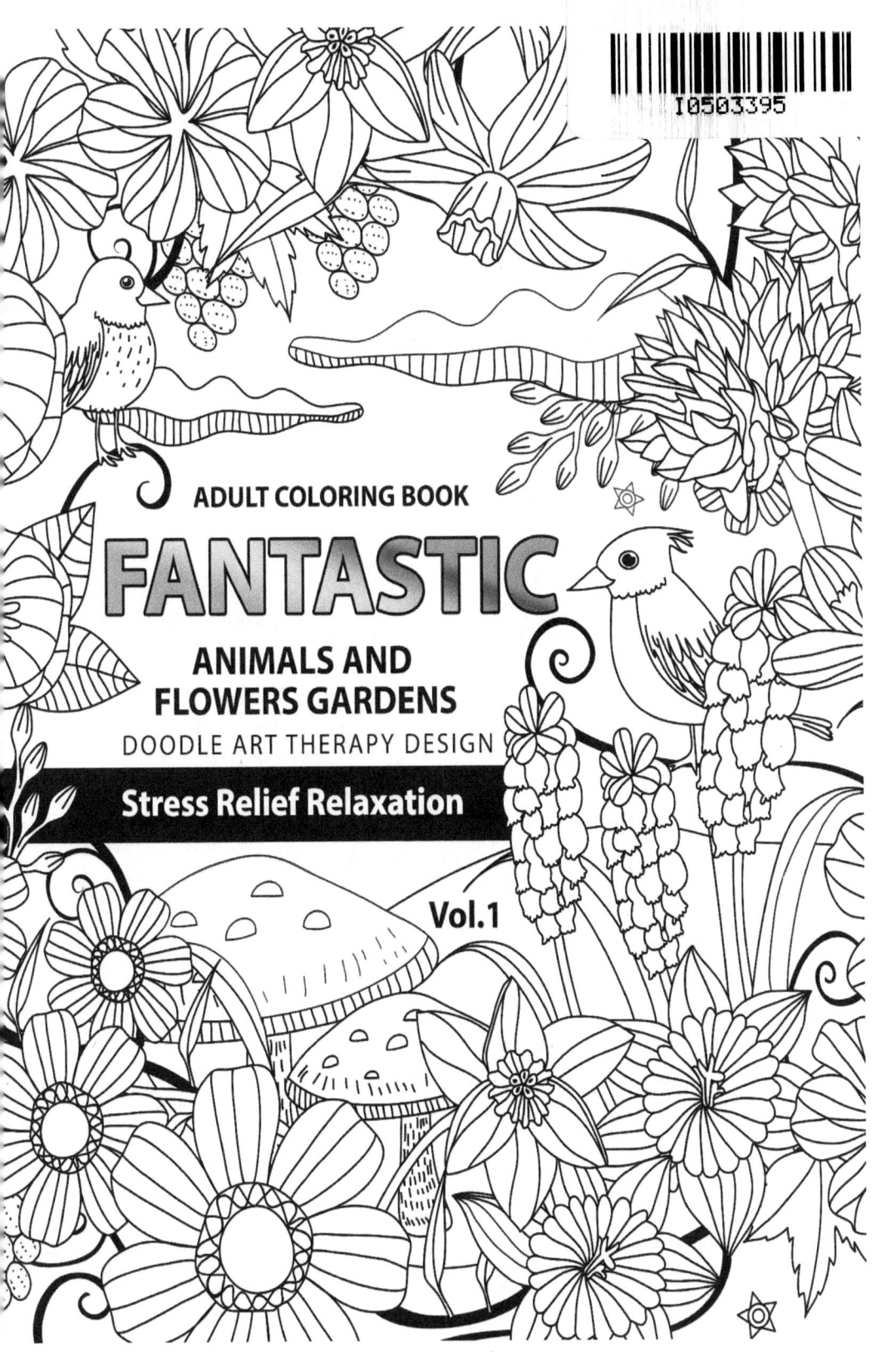

ADULT COLORING BOOK

FANTASTIC

ANIMALS AND
FLOWERS GARDENS

DOODLE ART THERAPY DESIGN

Stress Relief Relaxation

Vol.1

TEST YOUR COLOR

TEST YOUR COLOR

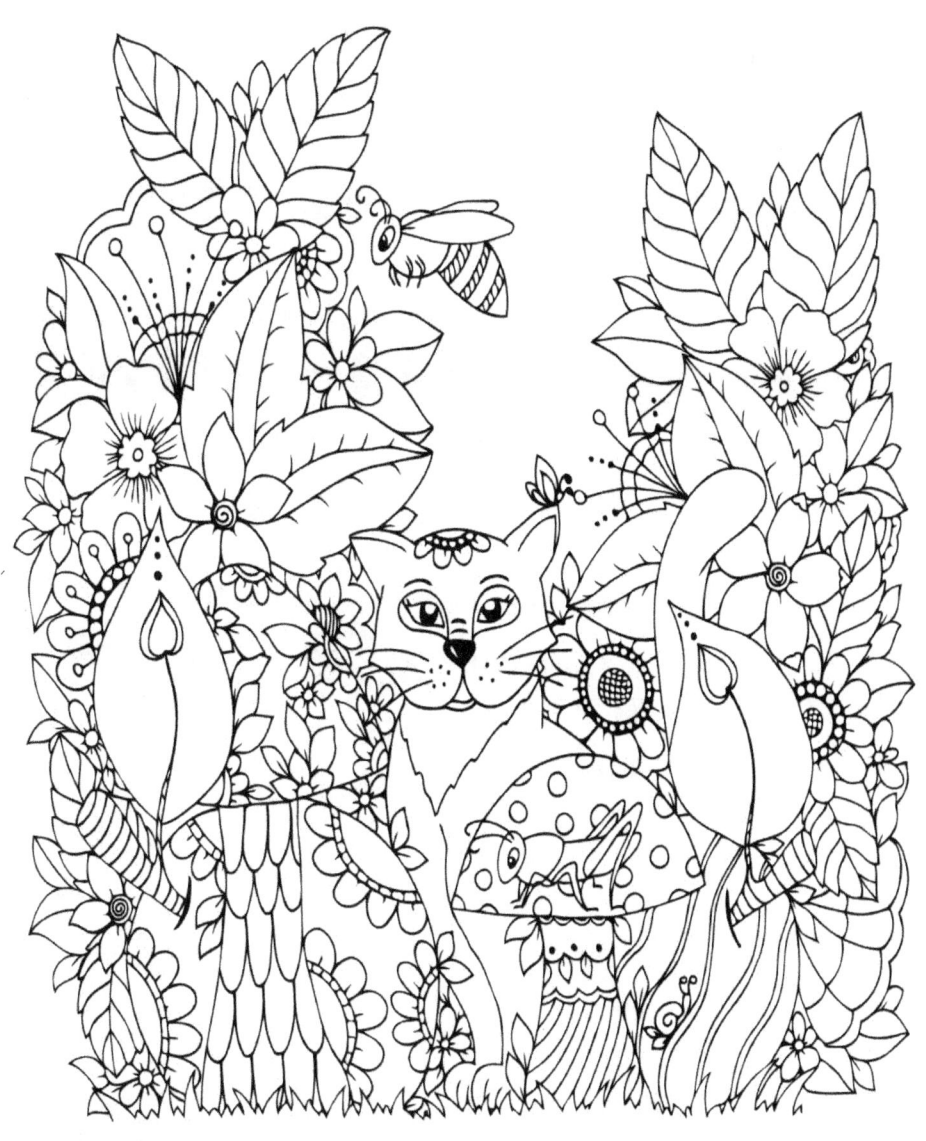

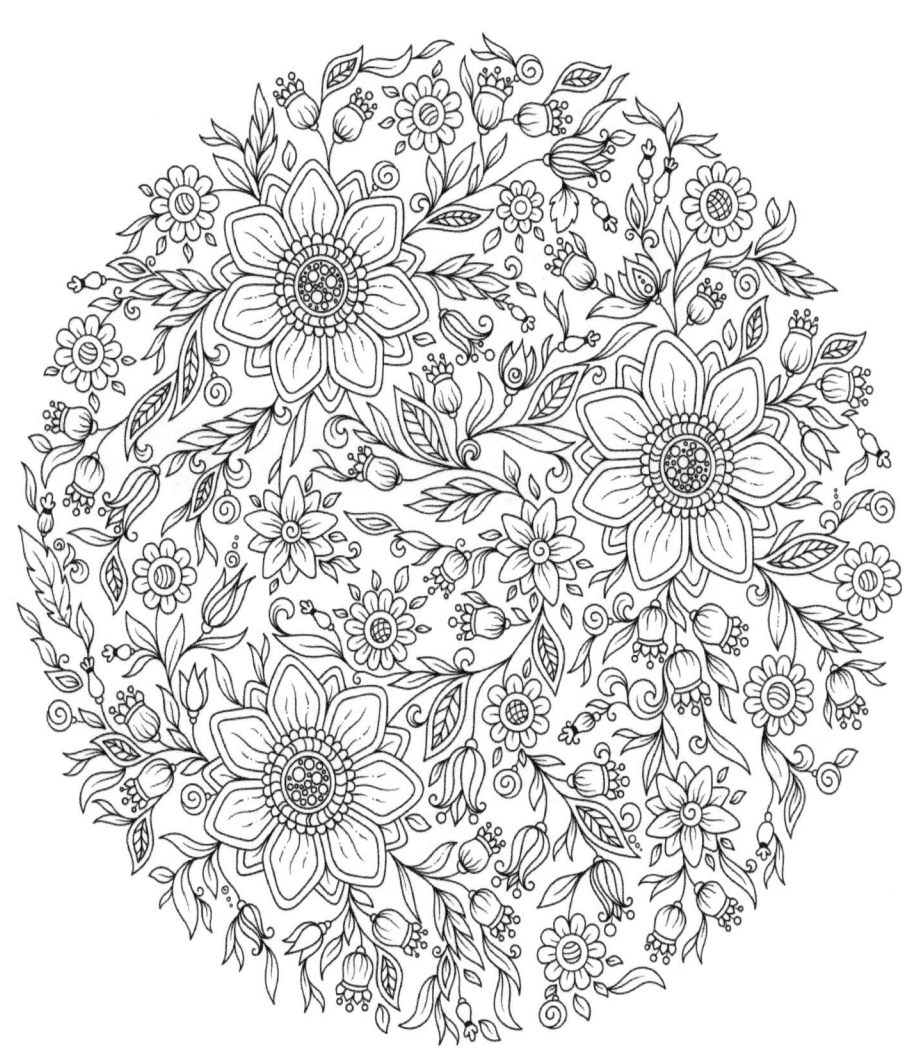

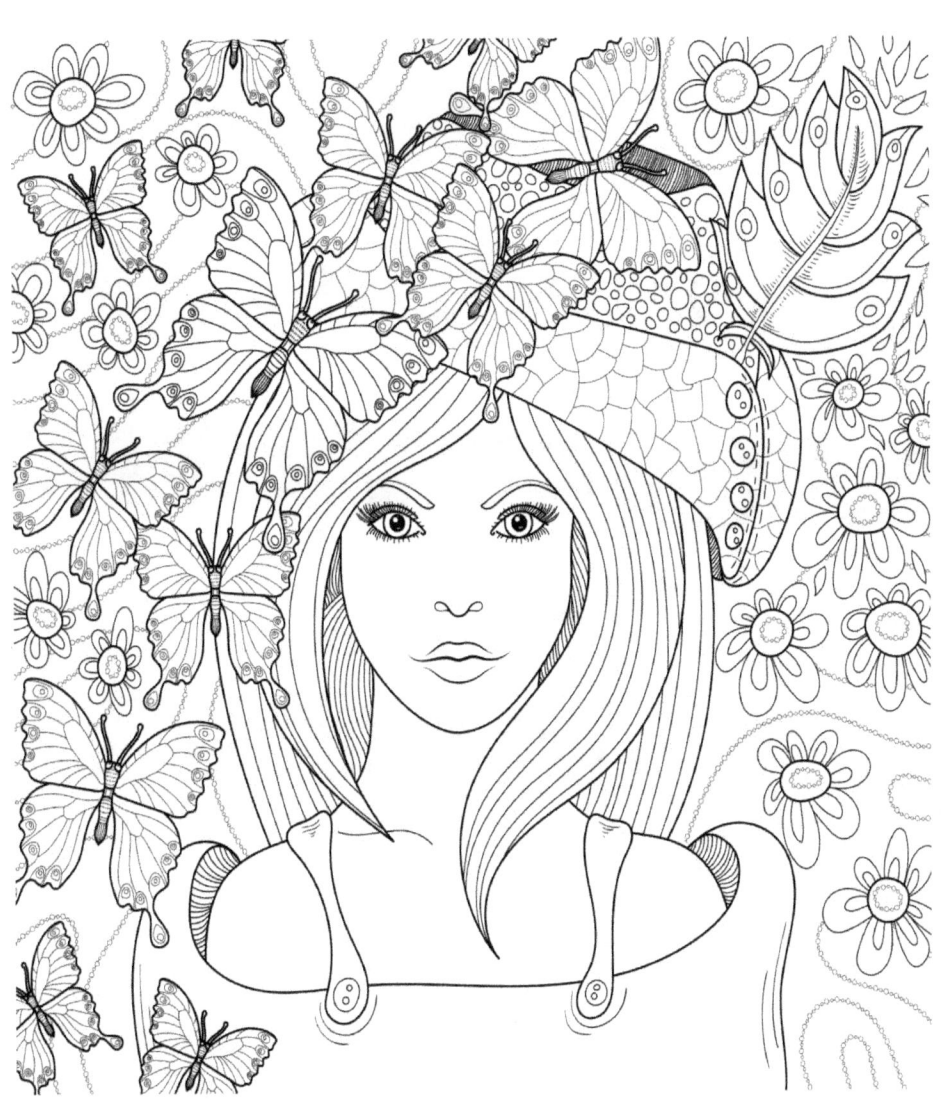

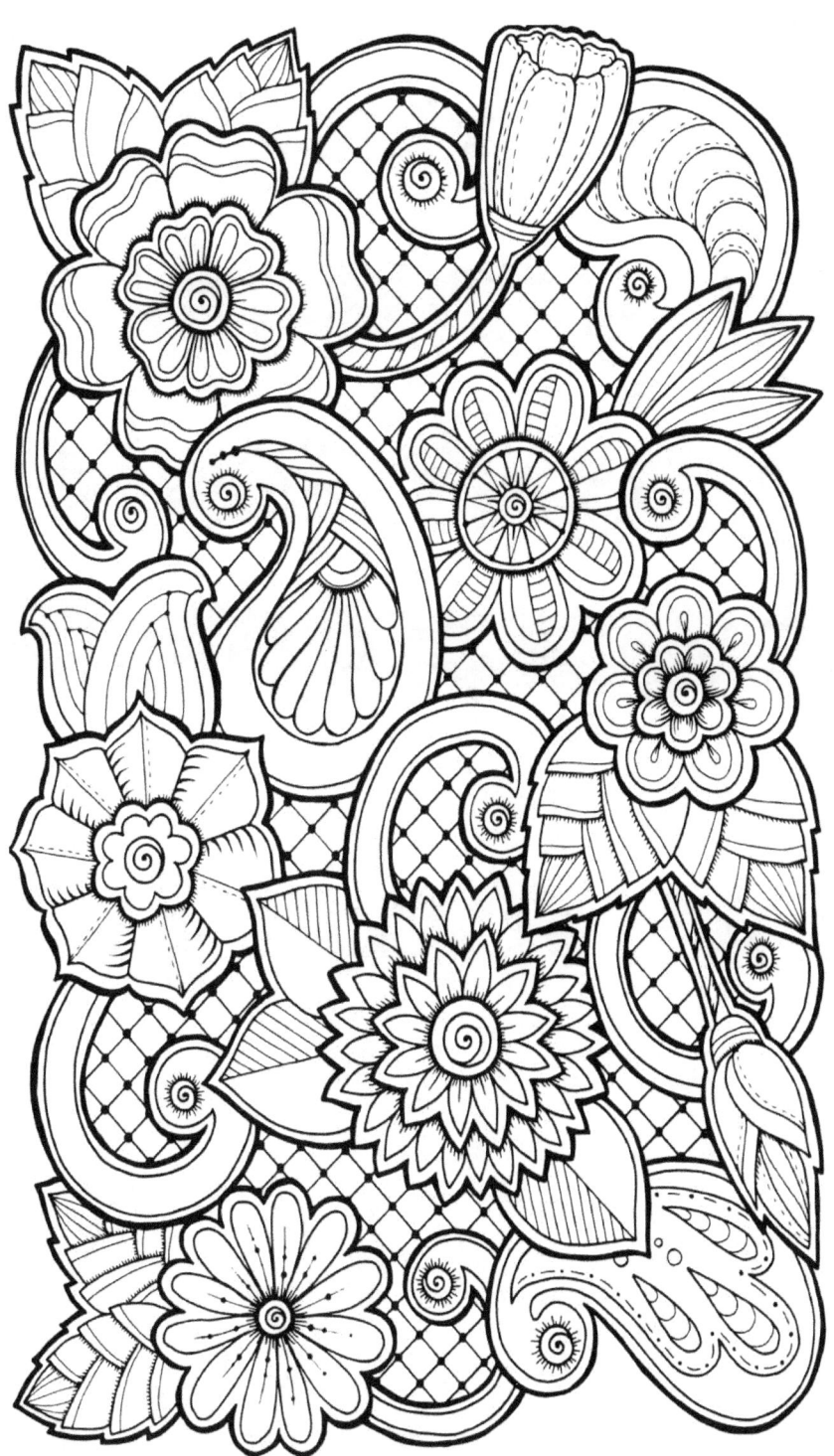

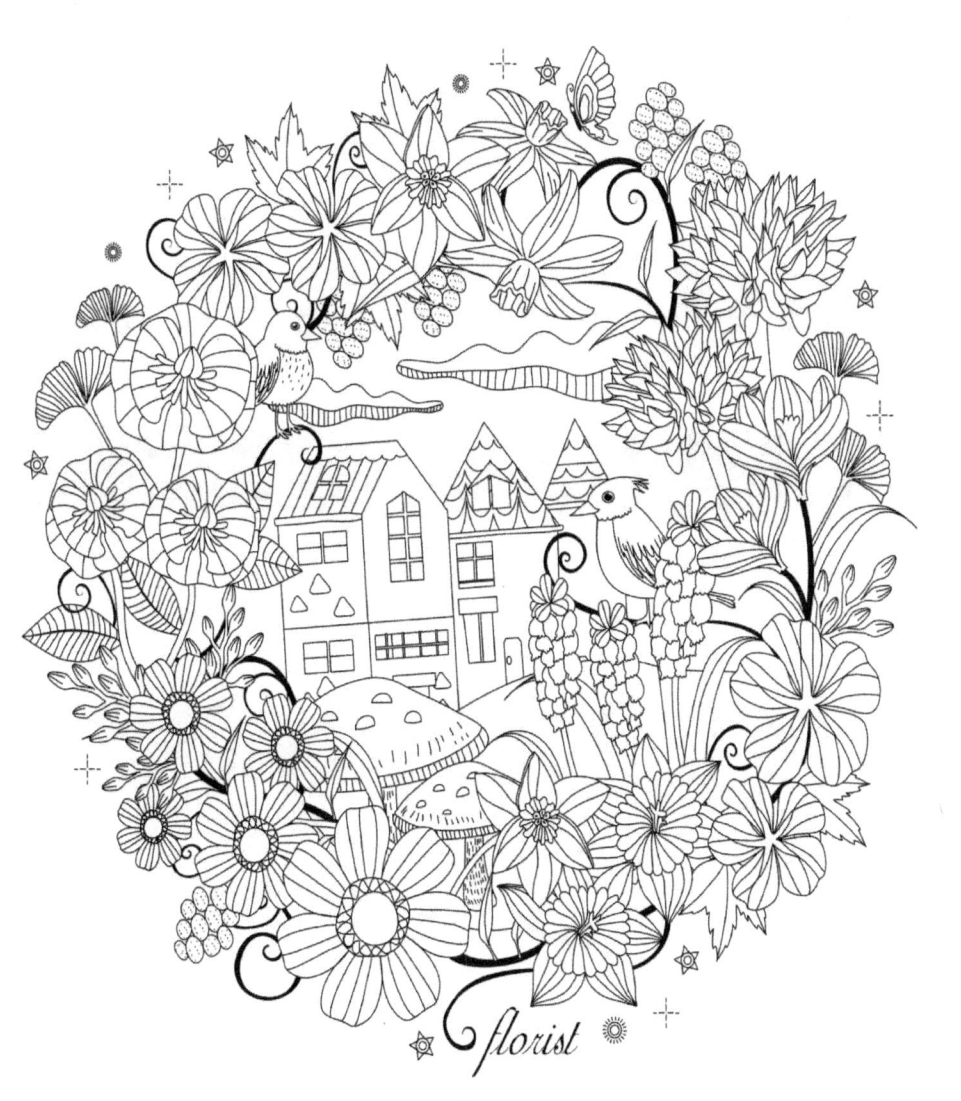

florist

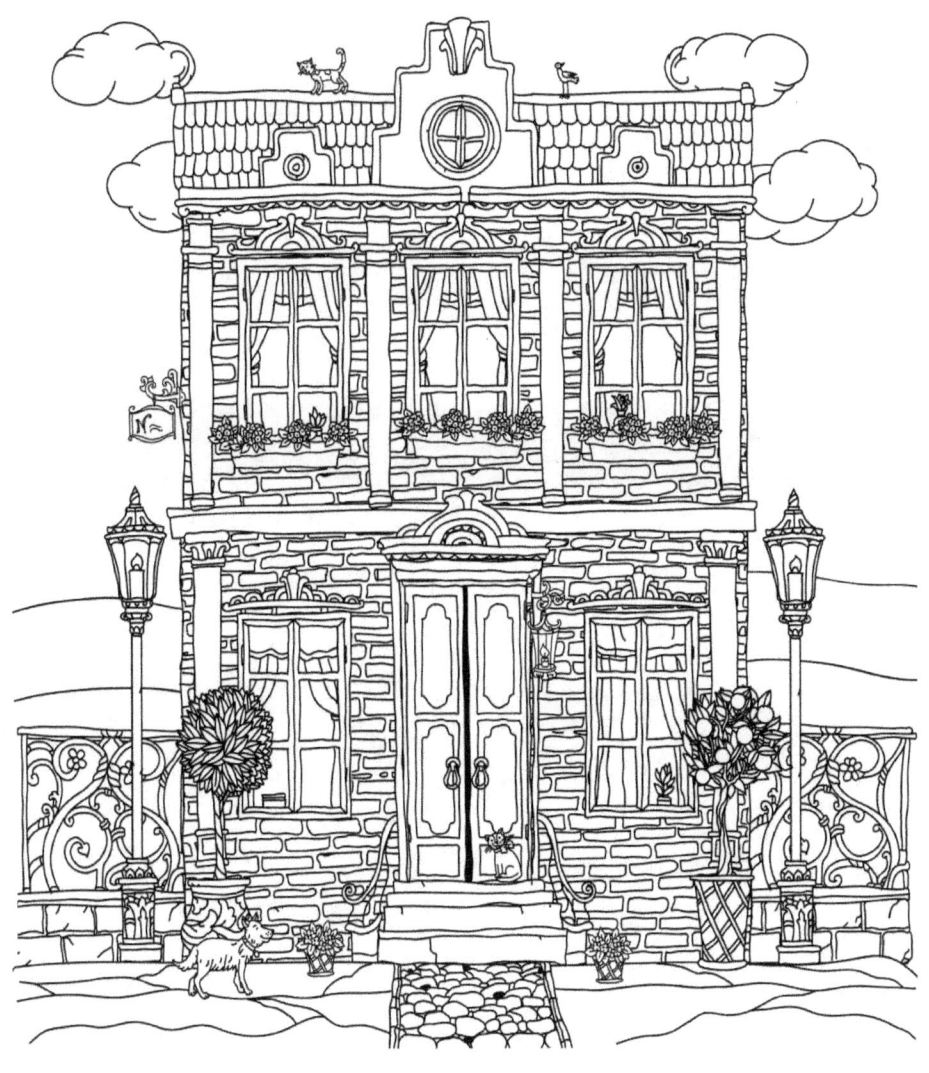

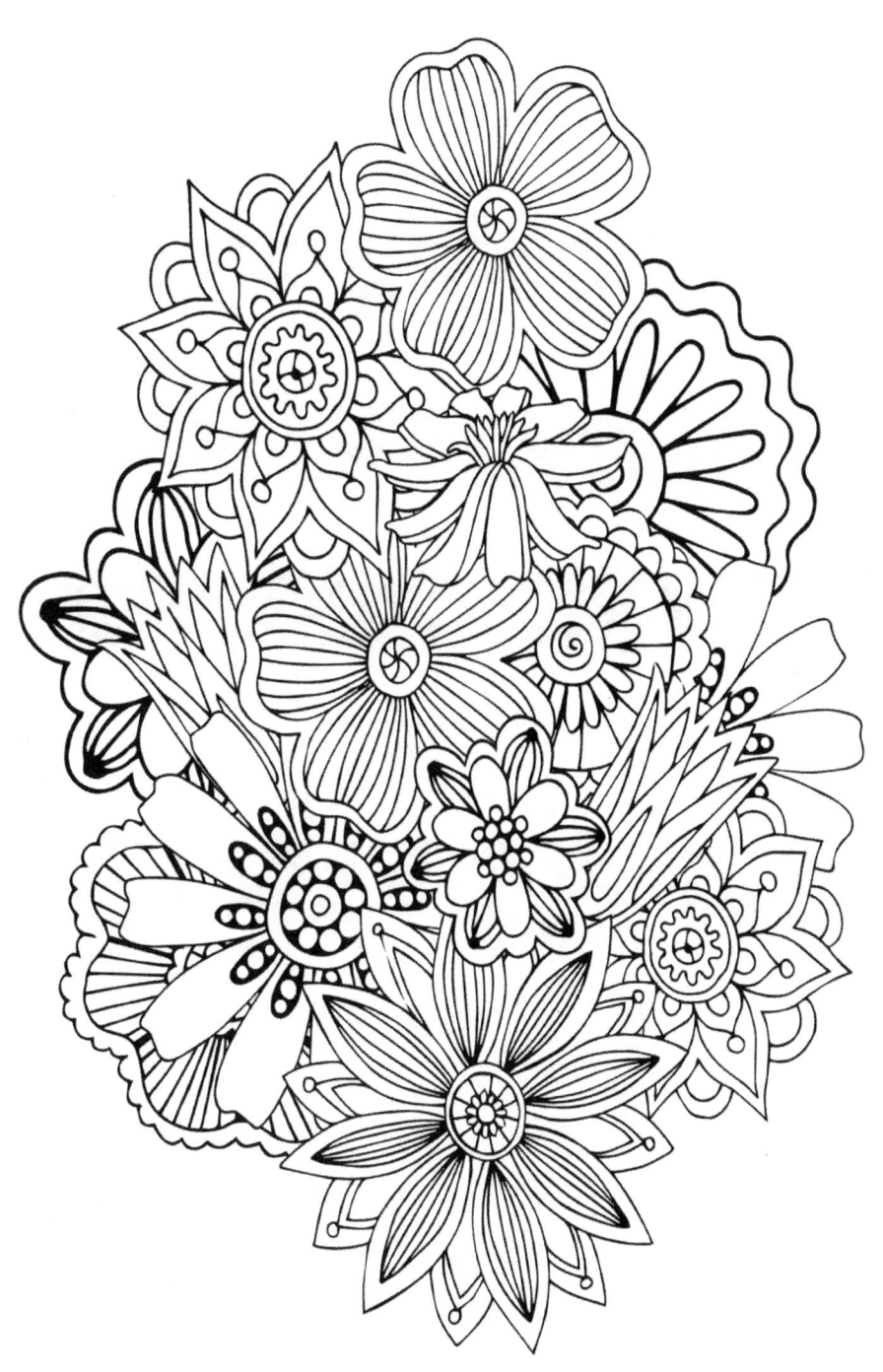

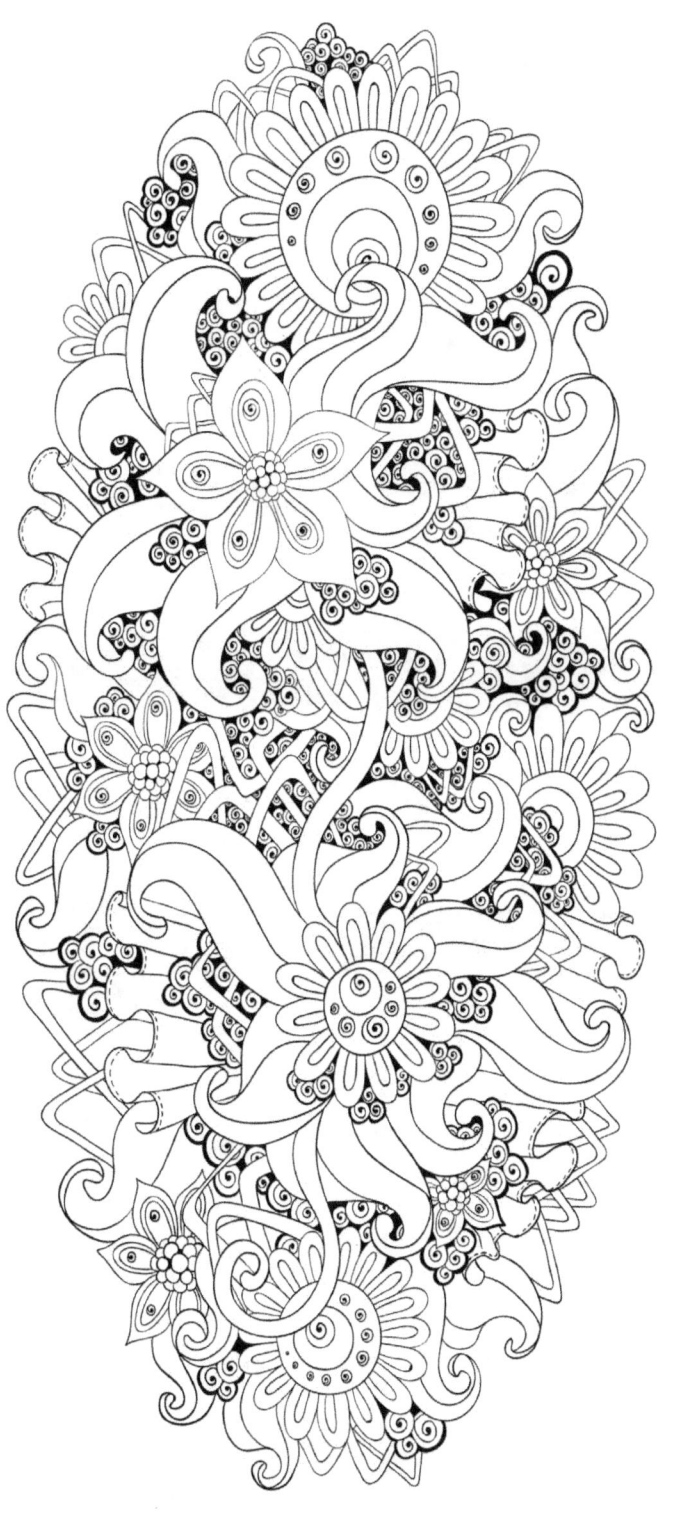

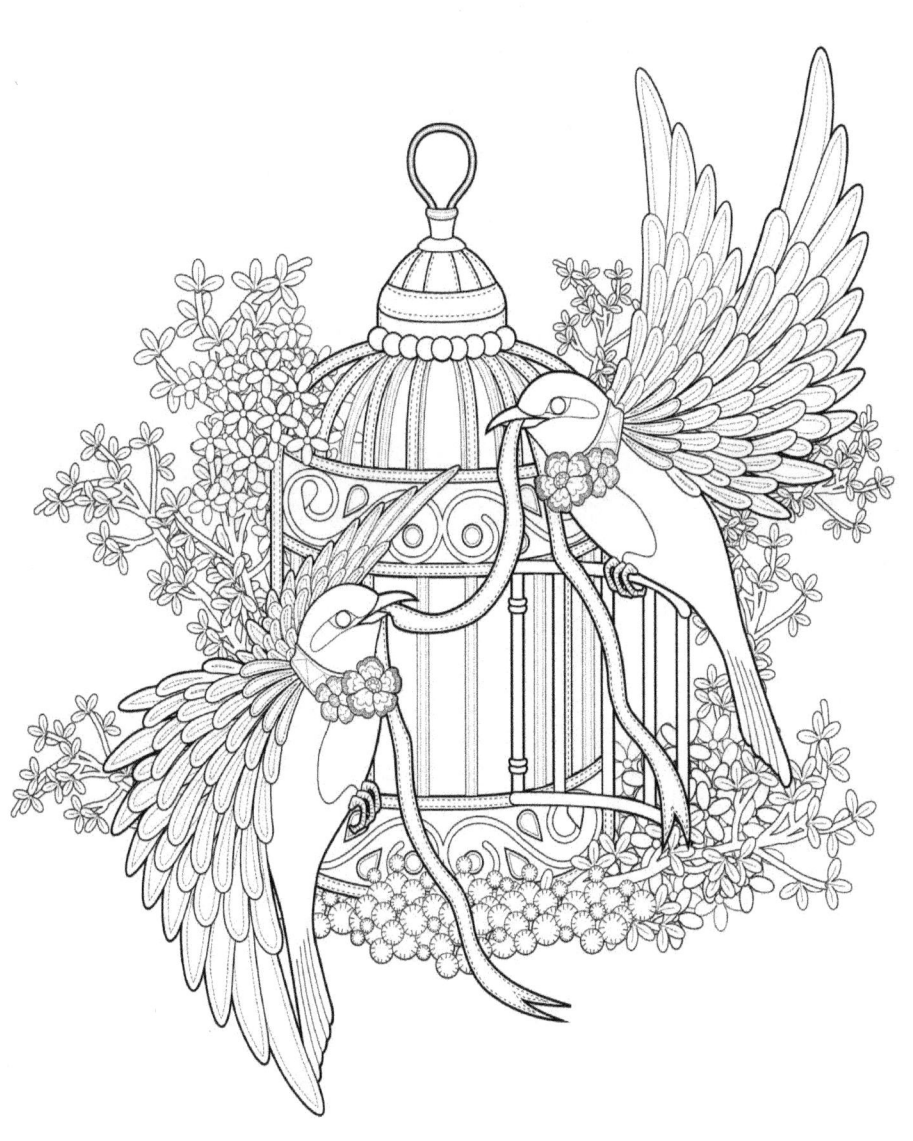

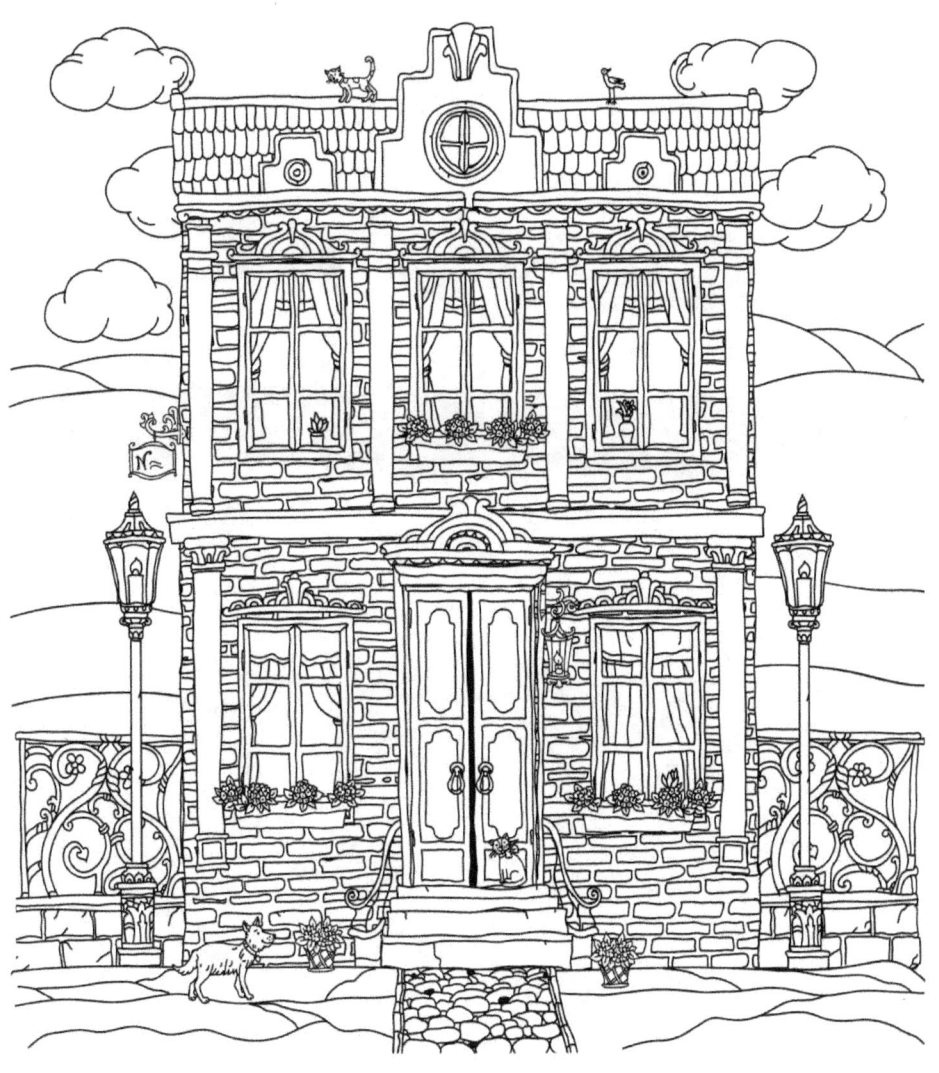

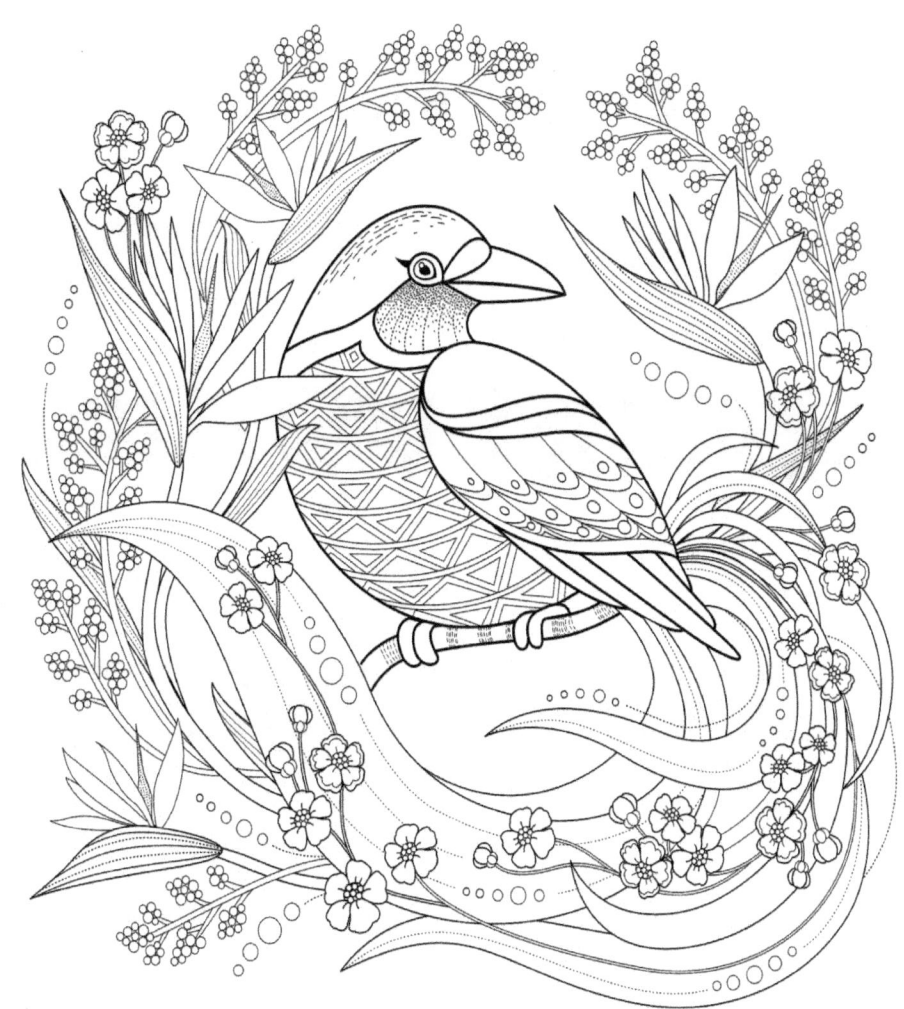

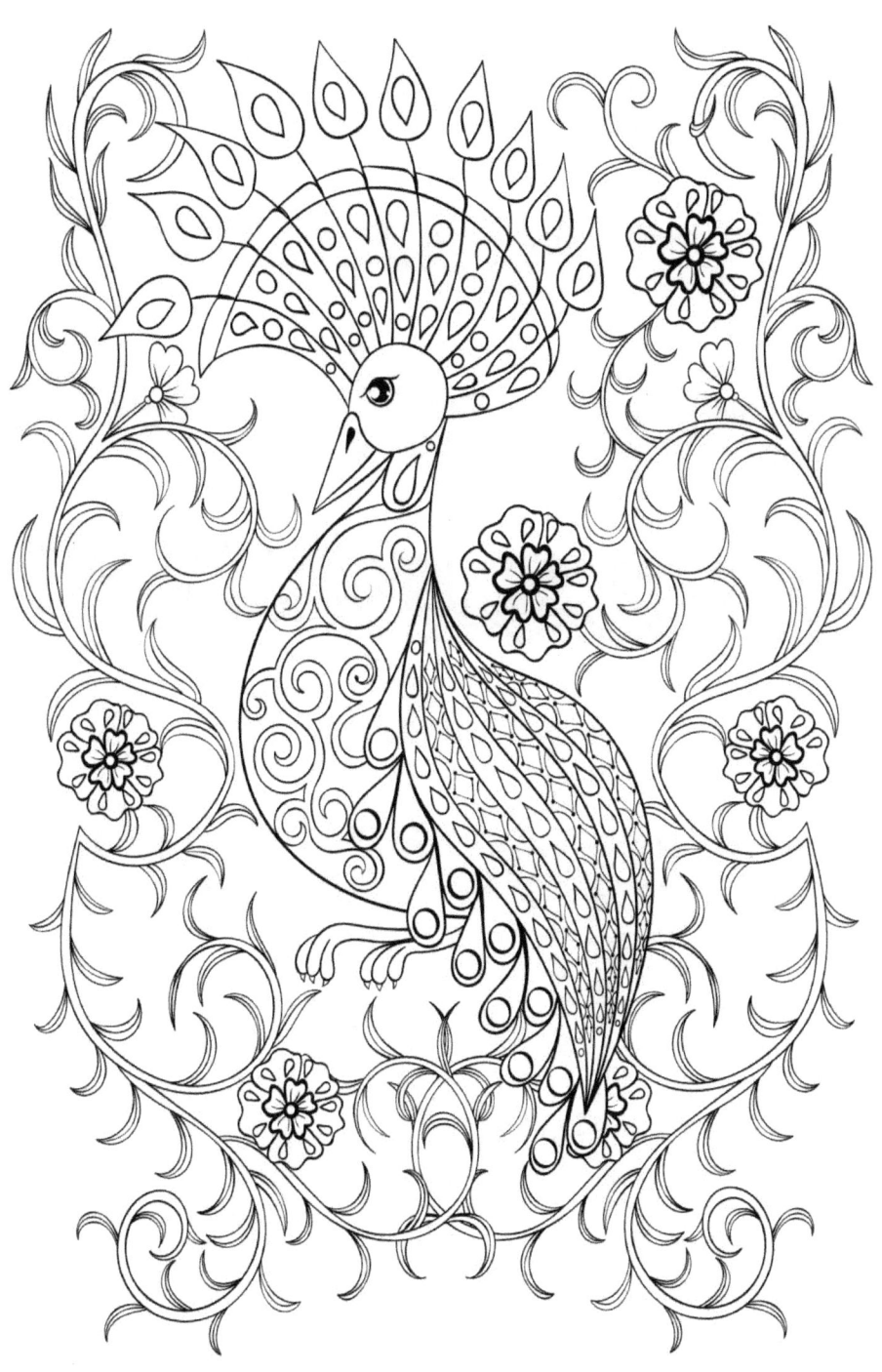

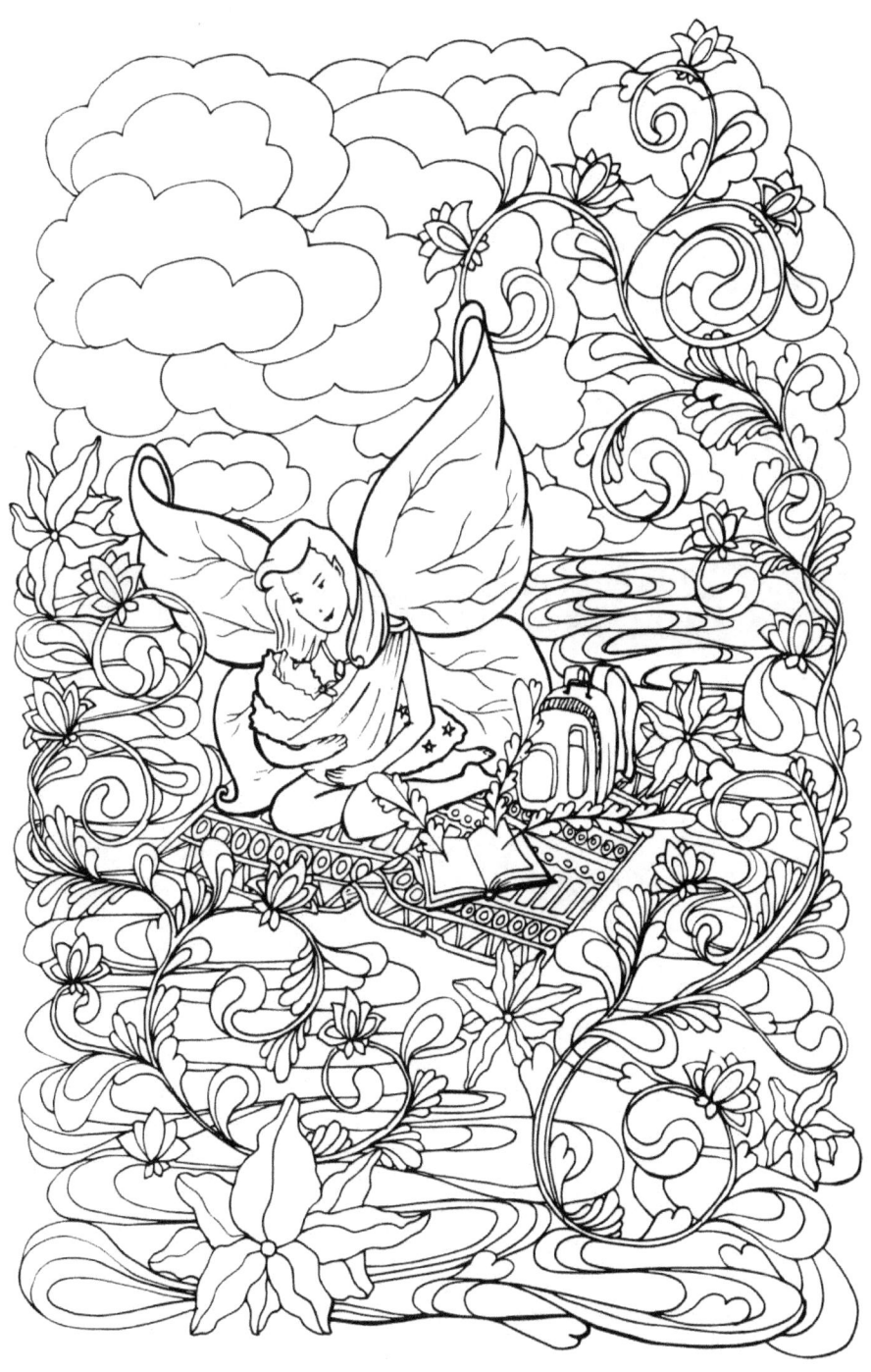

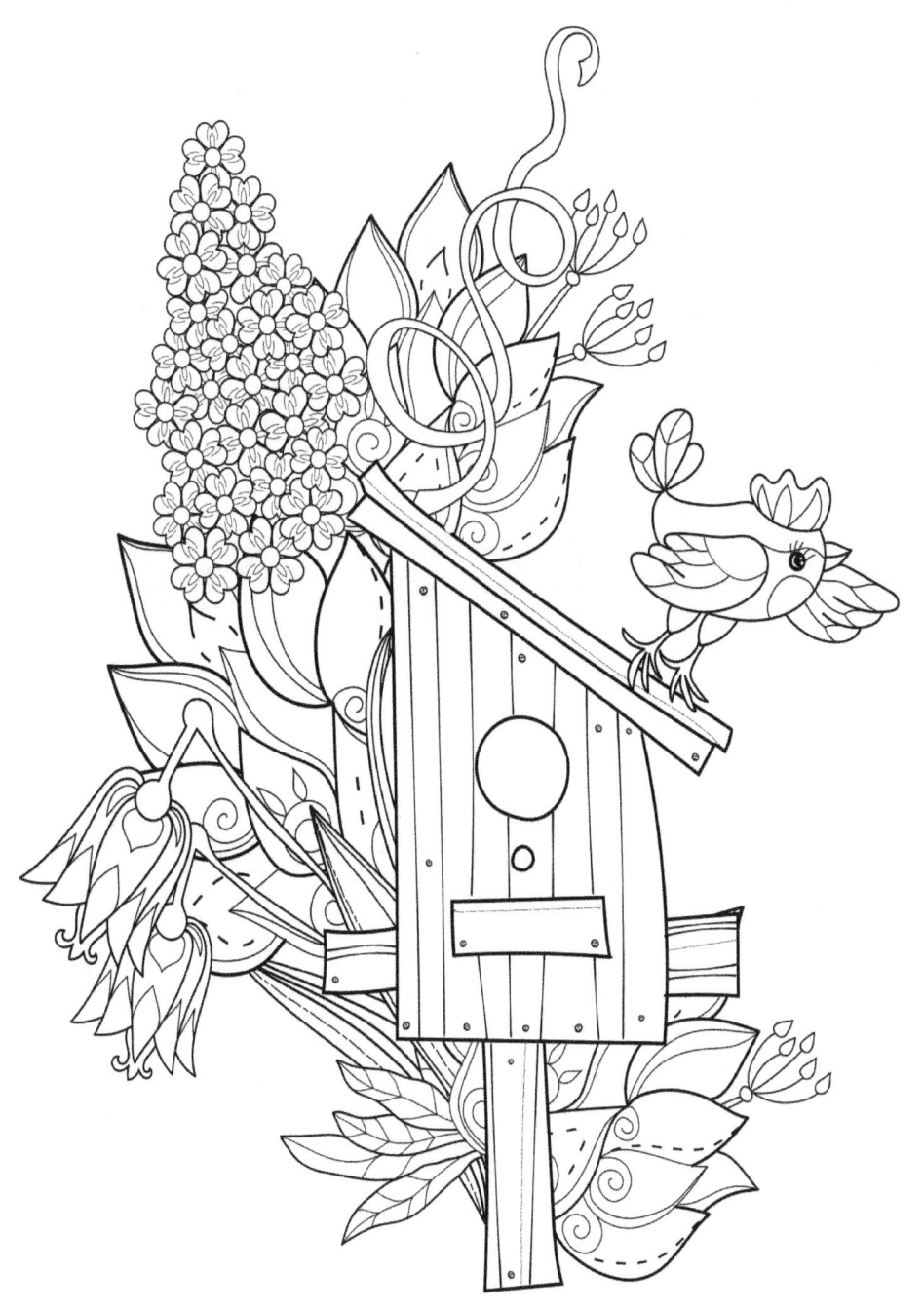

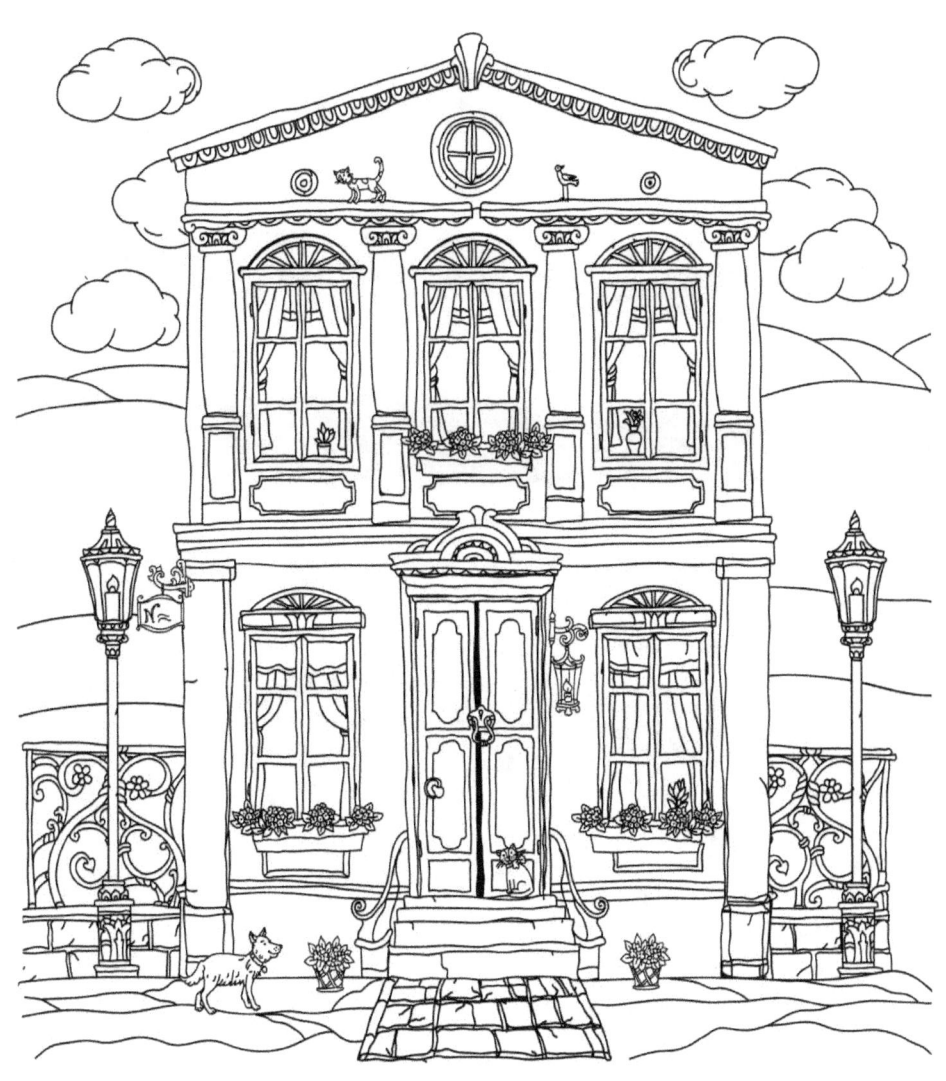

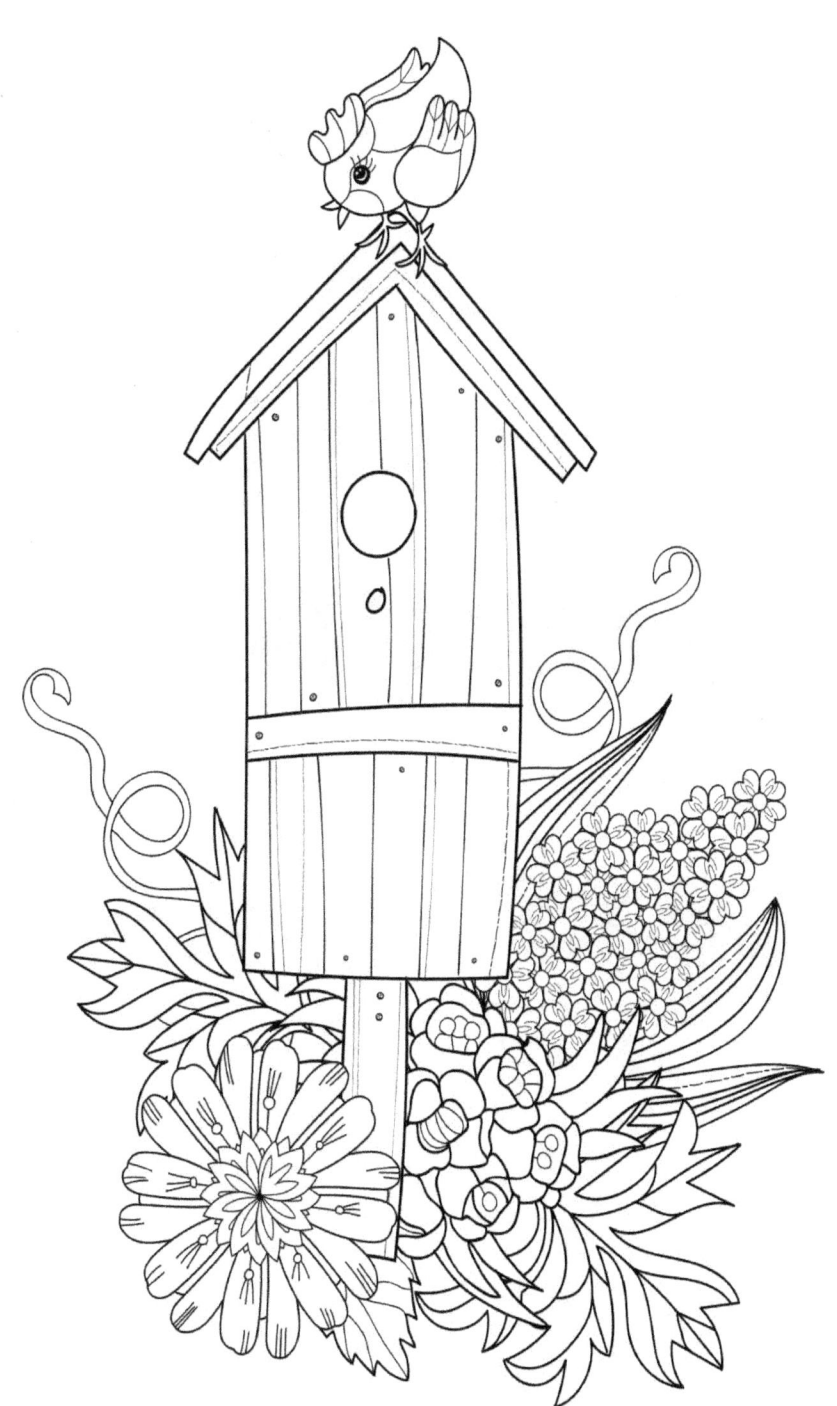

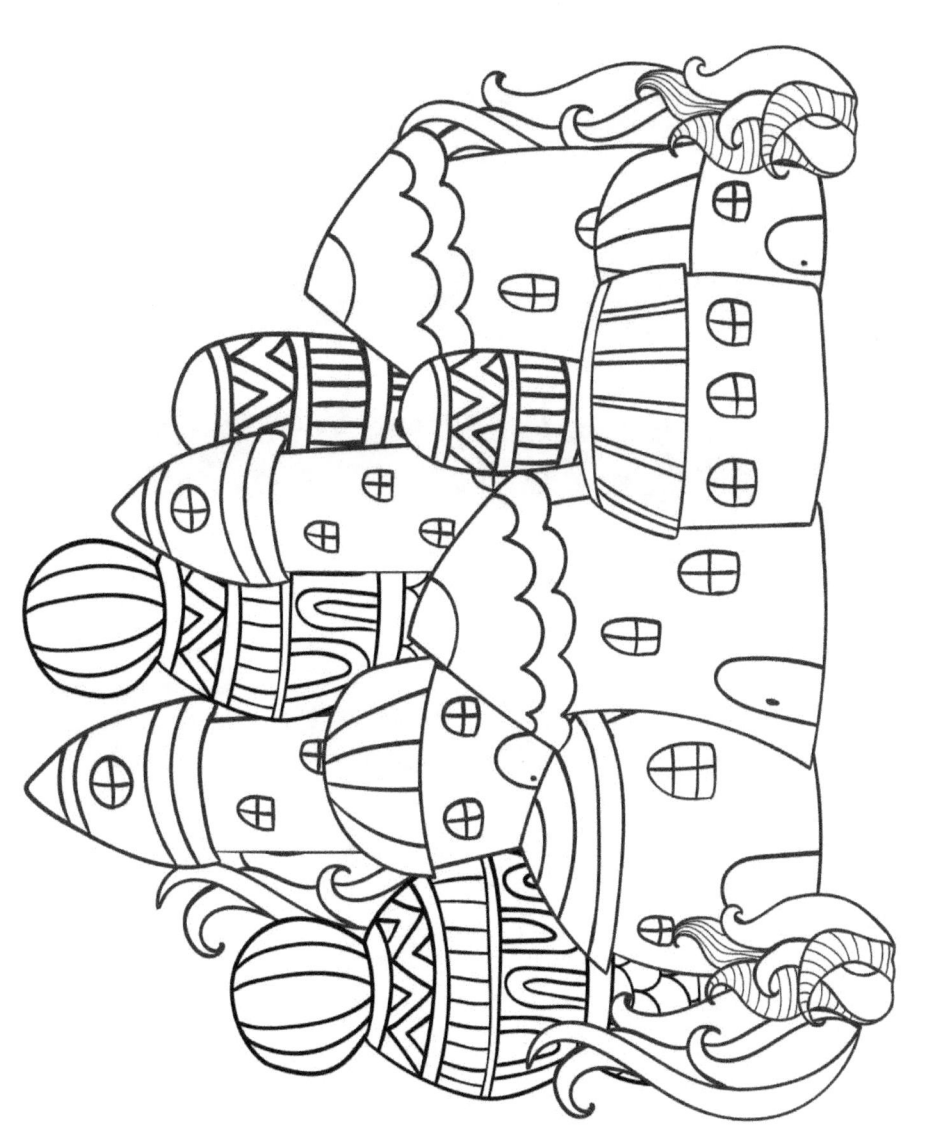

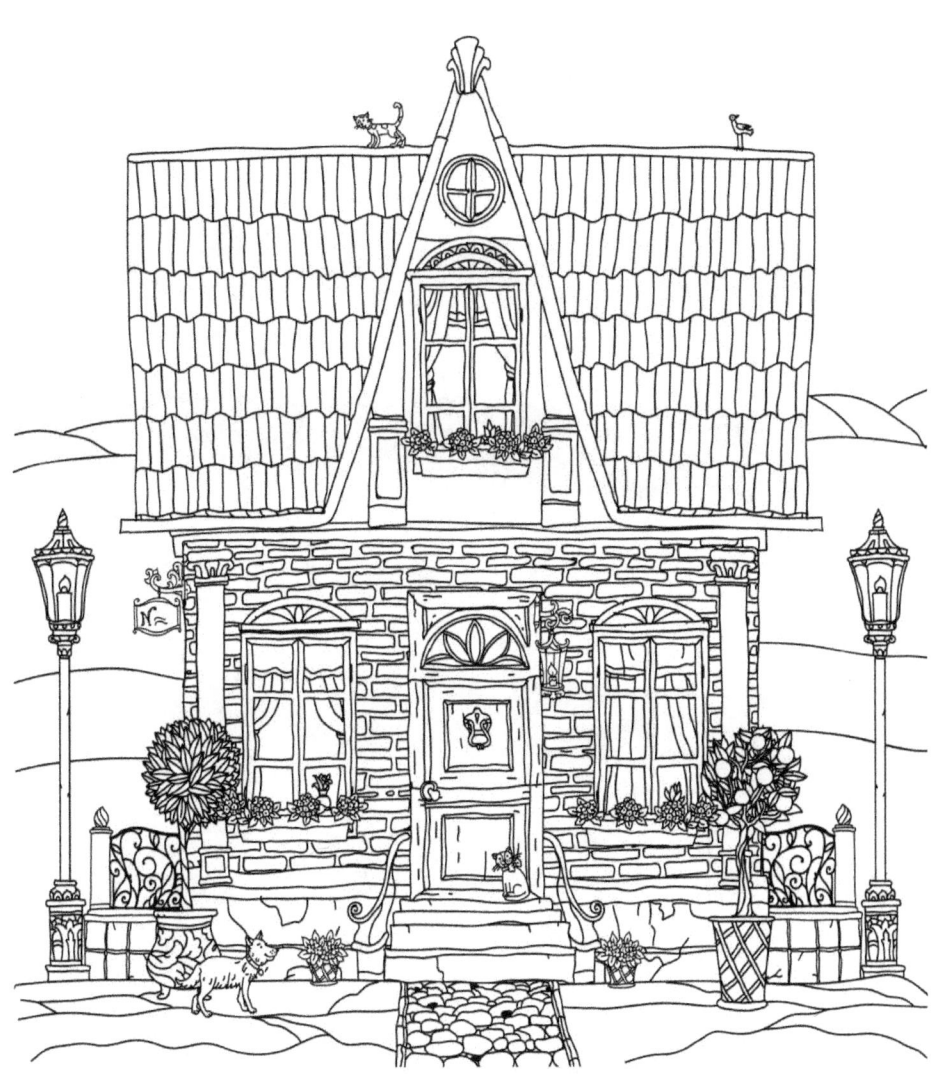

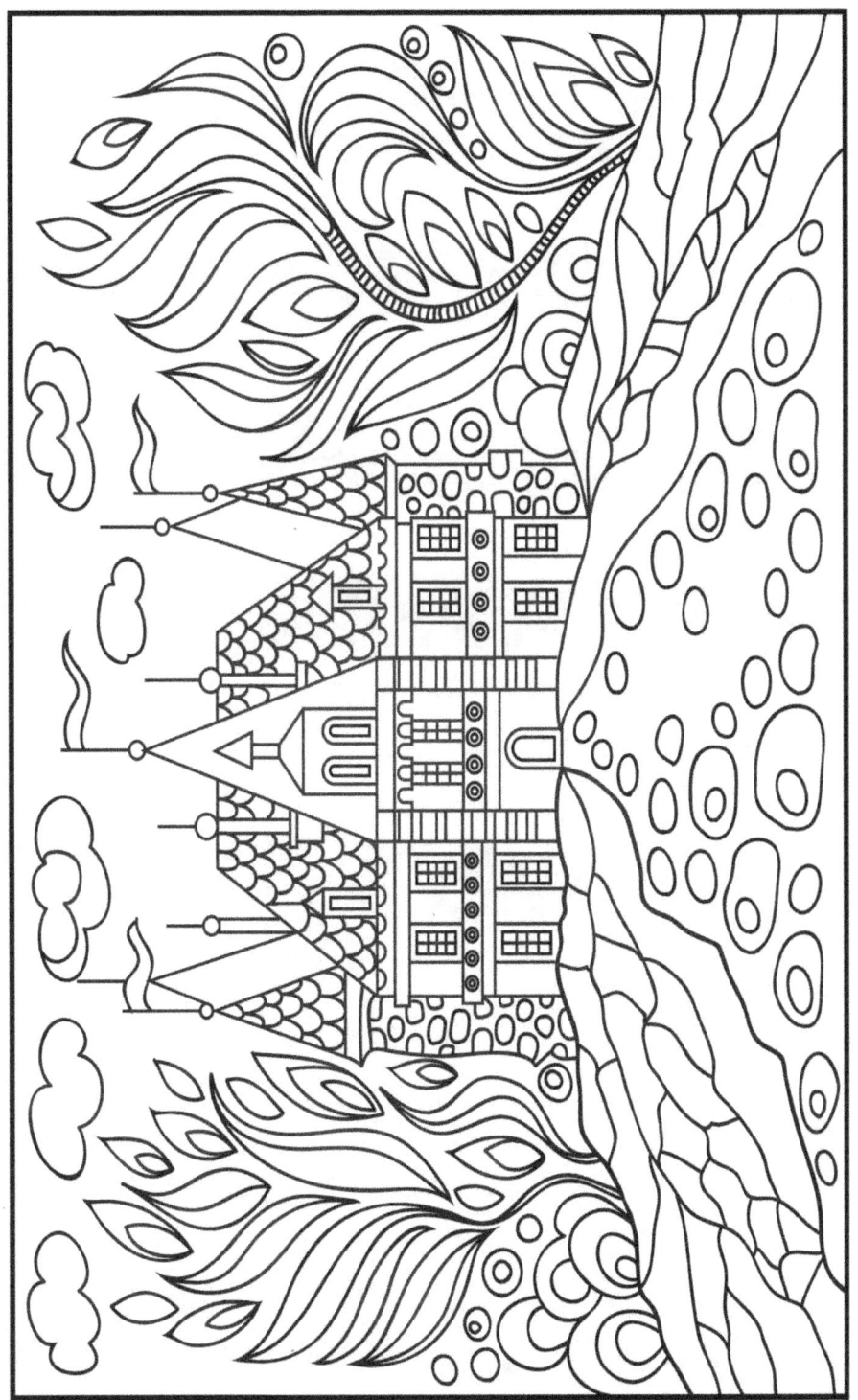

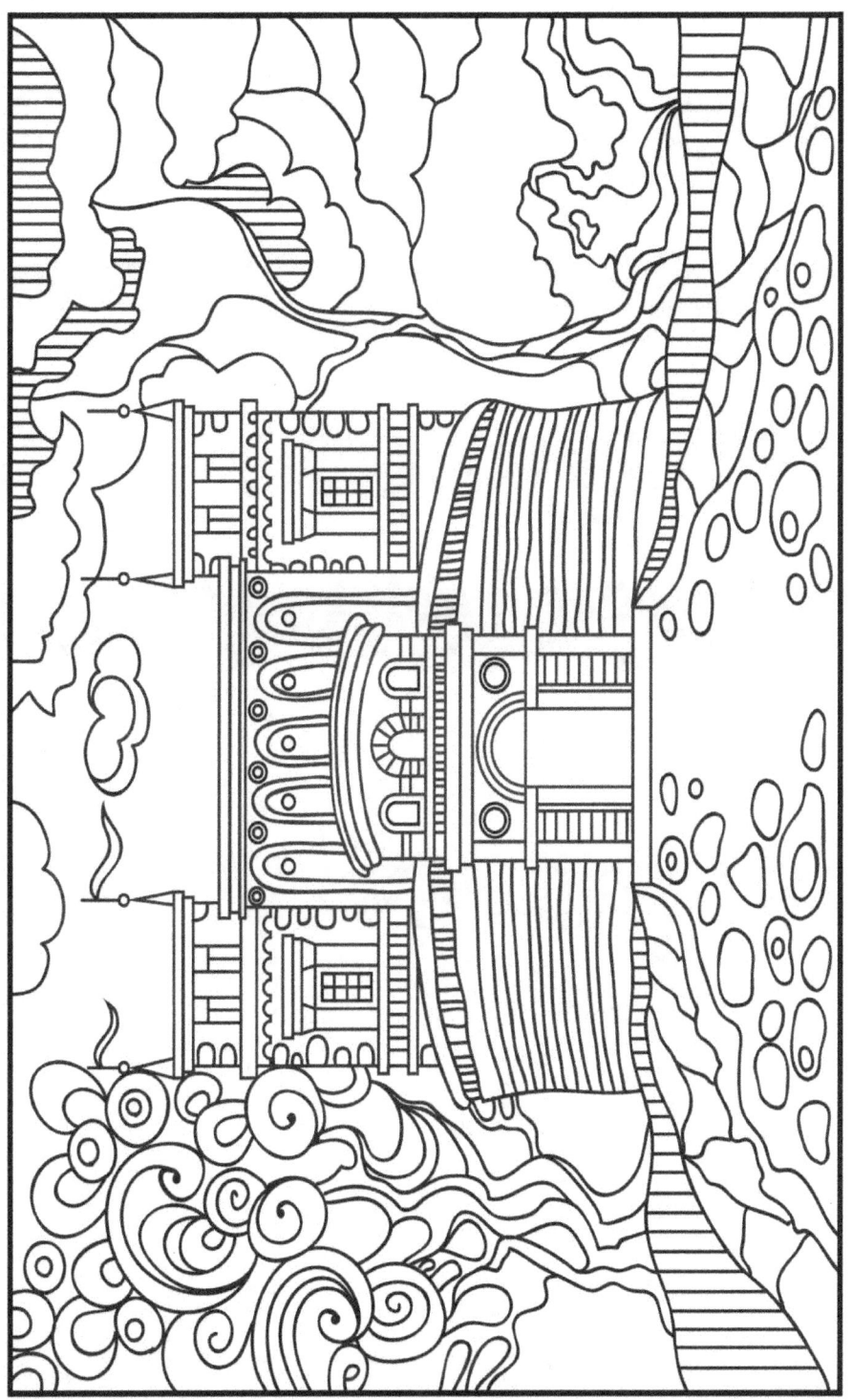

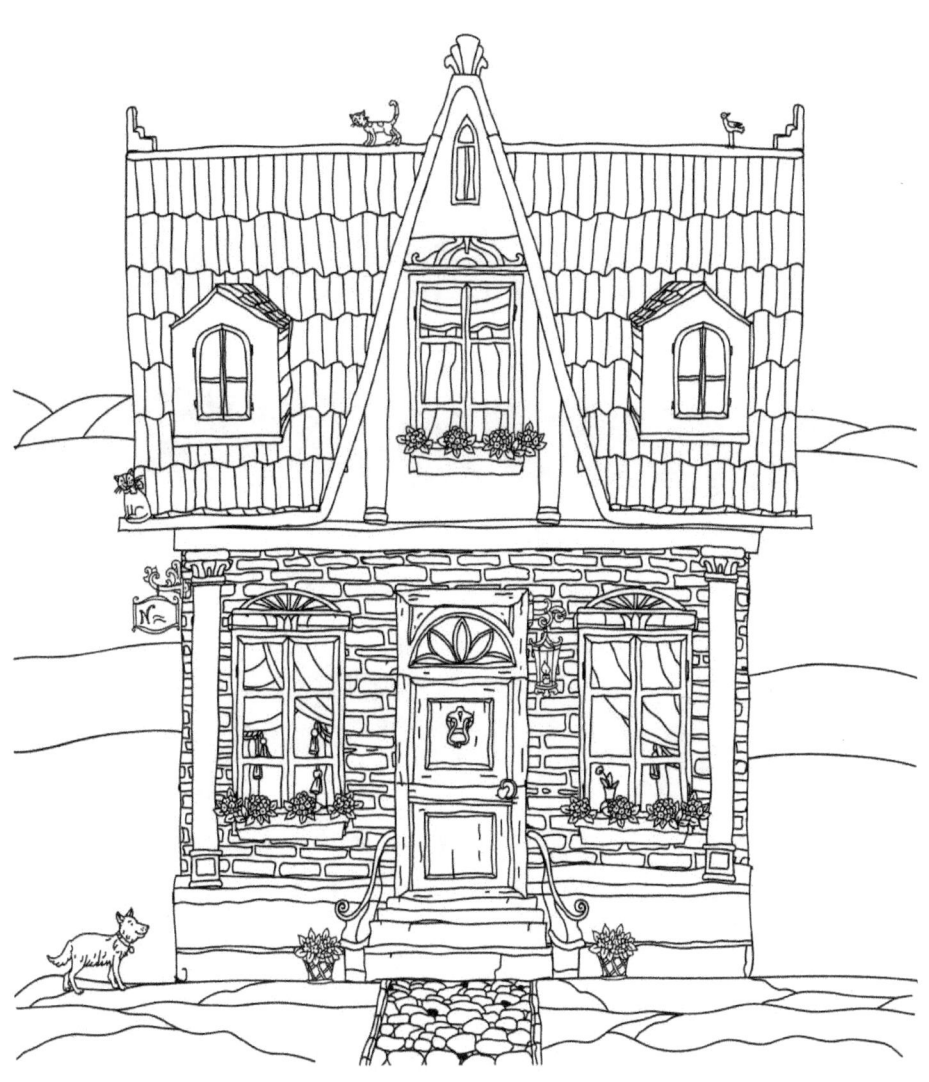

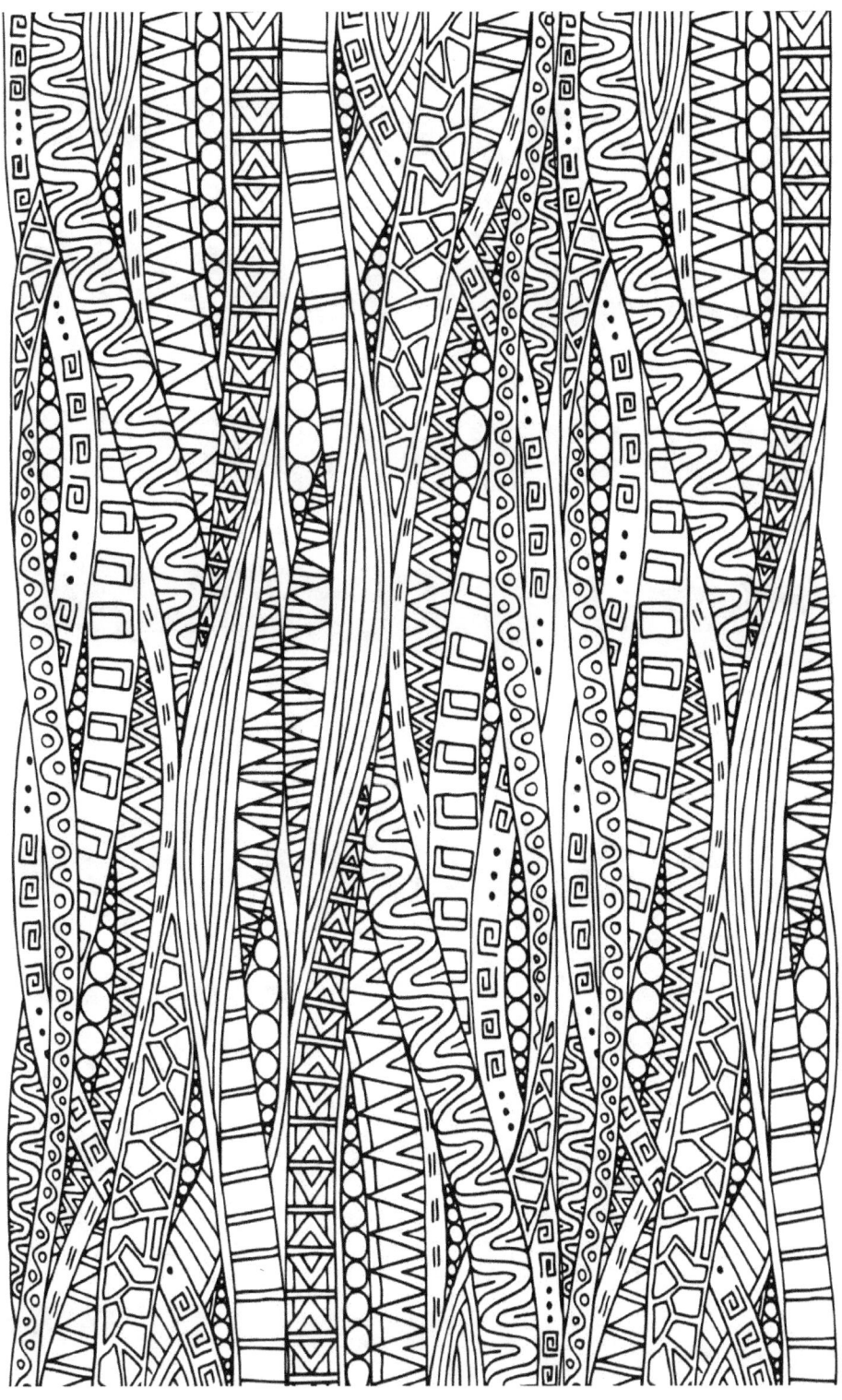

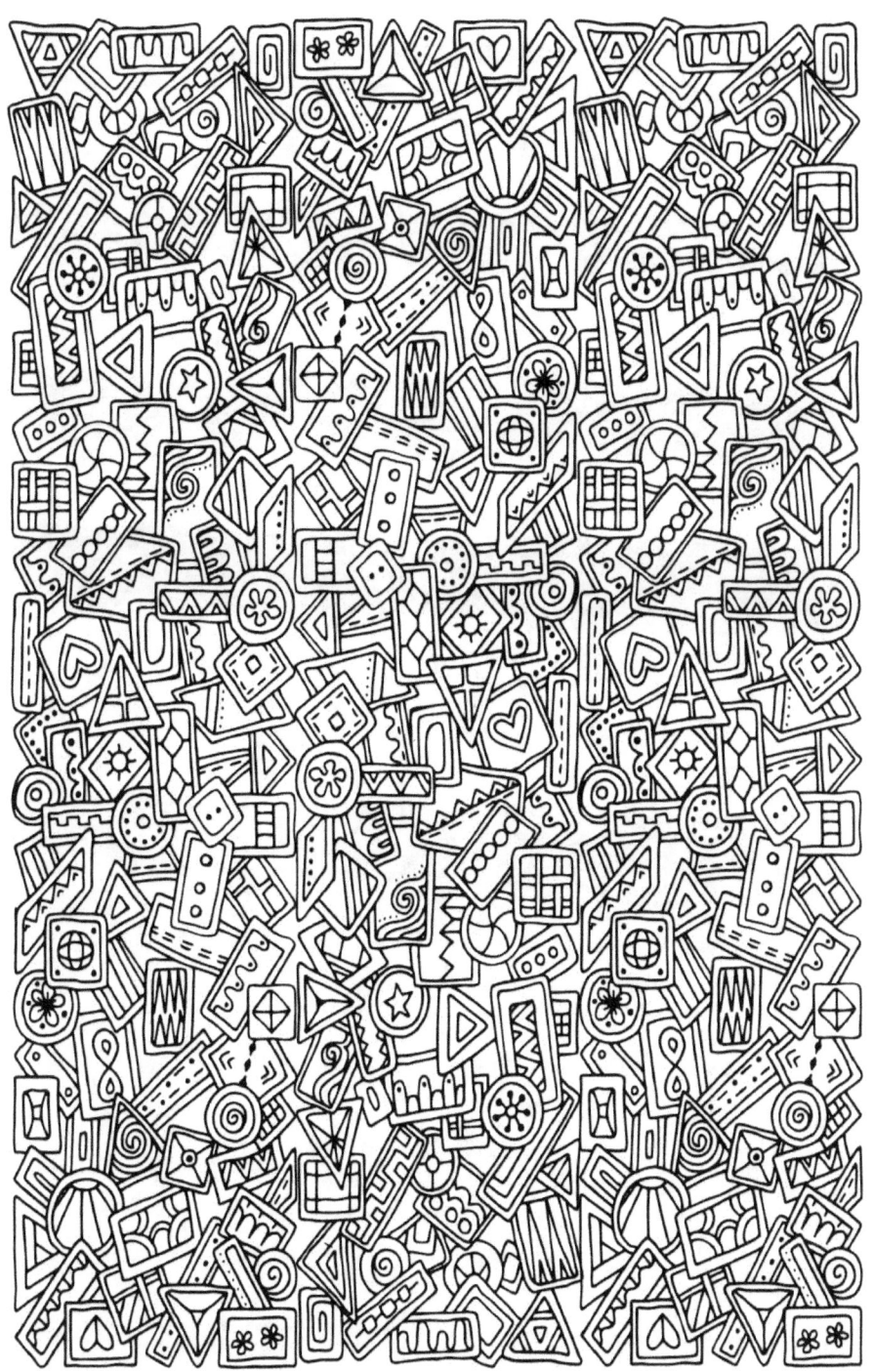

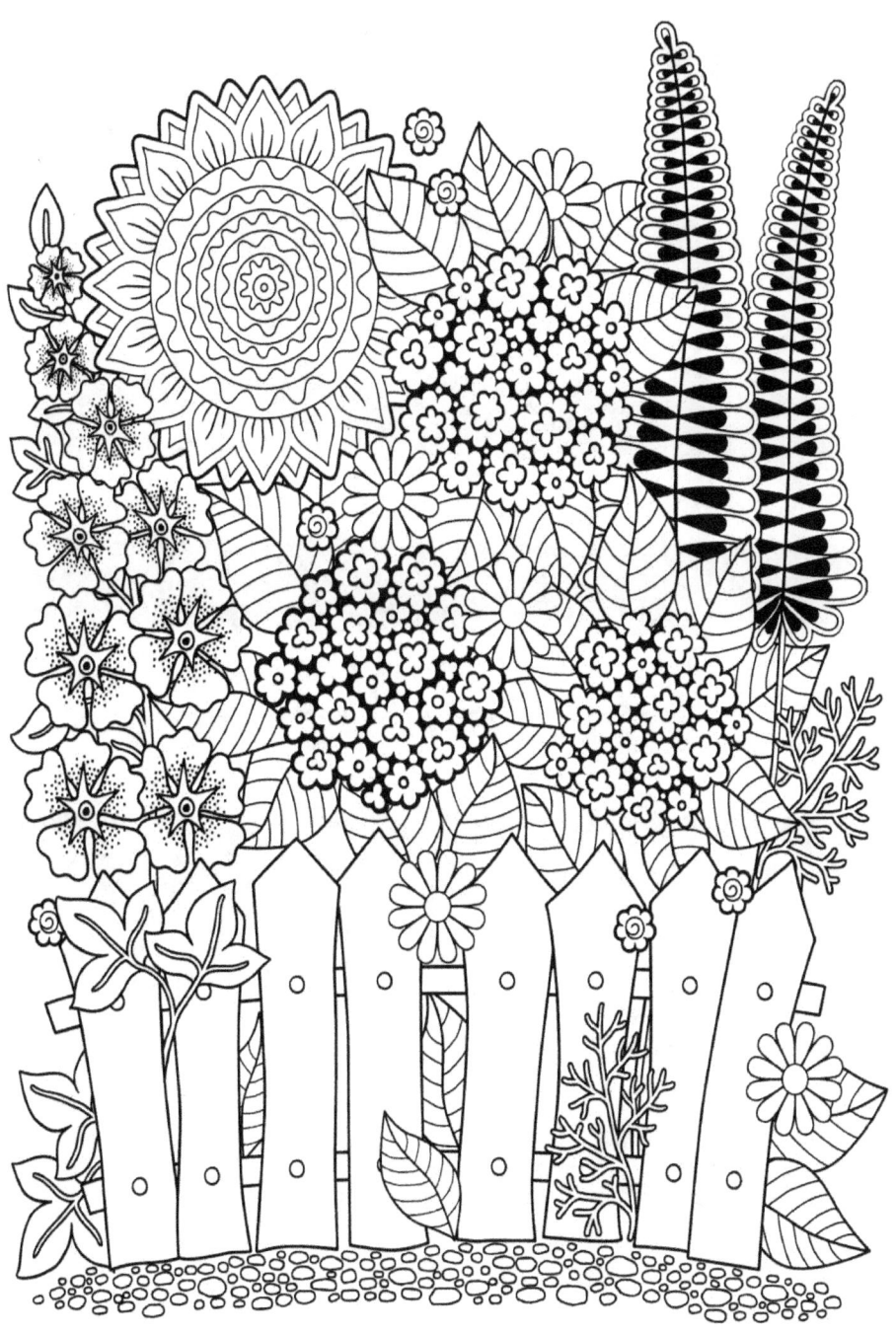

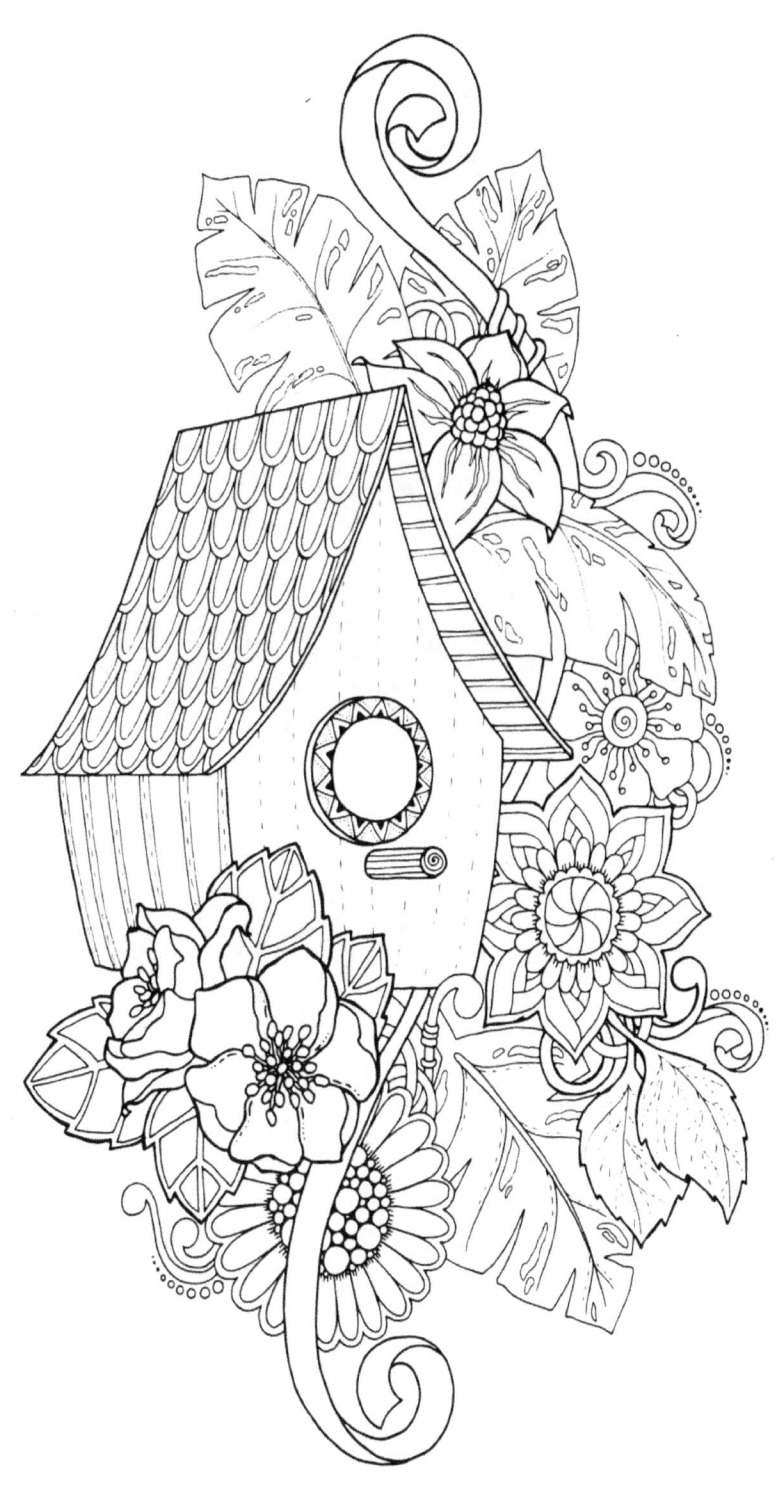

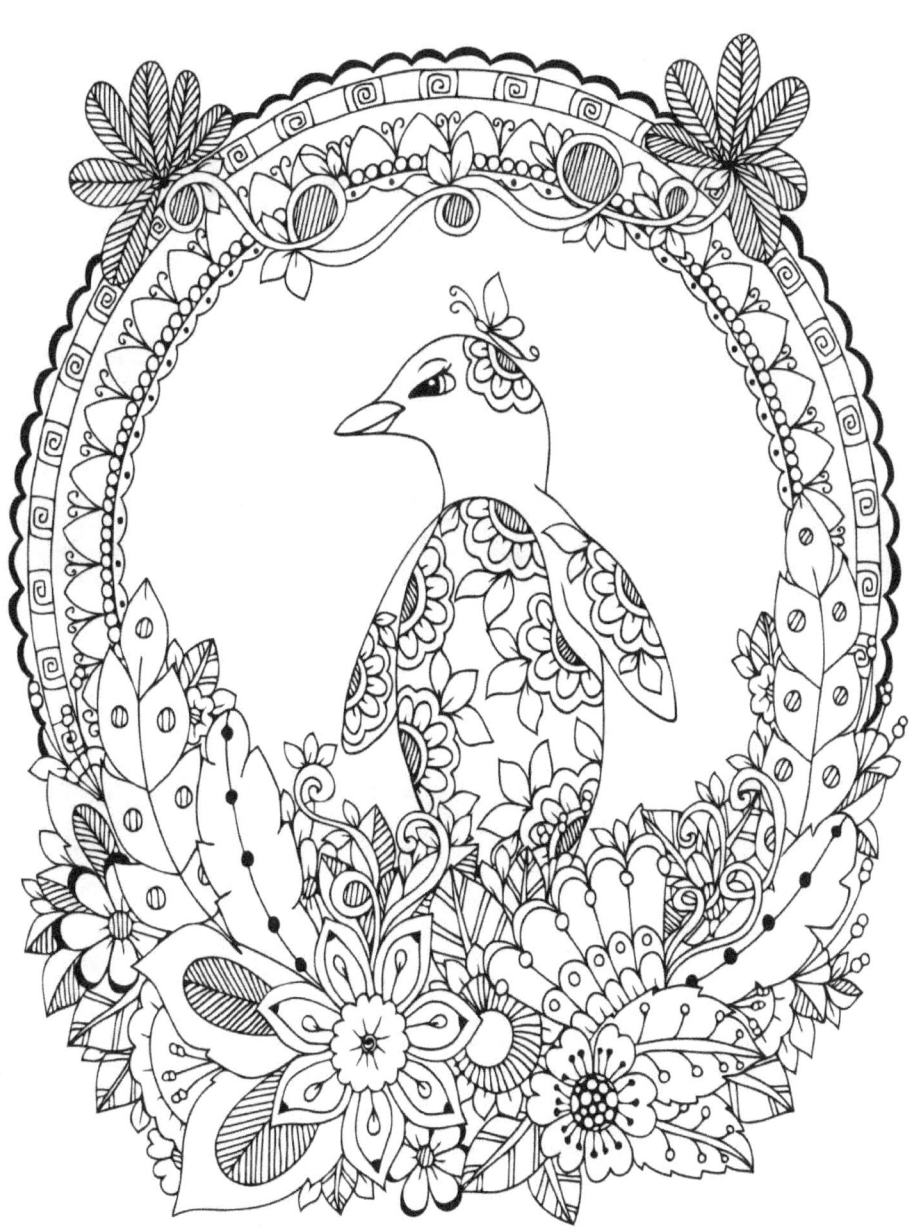

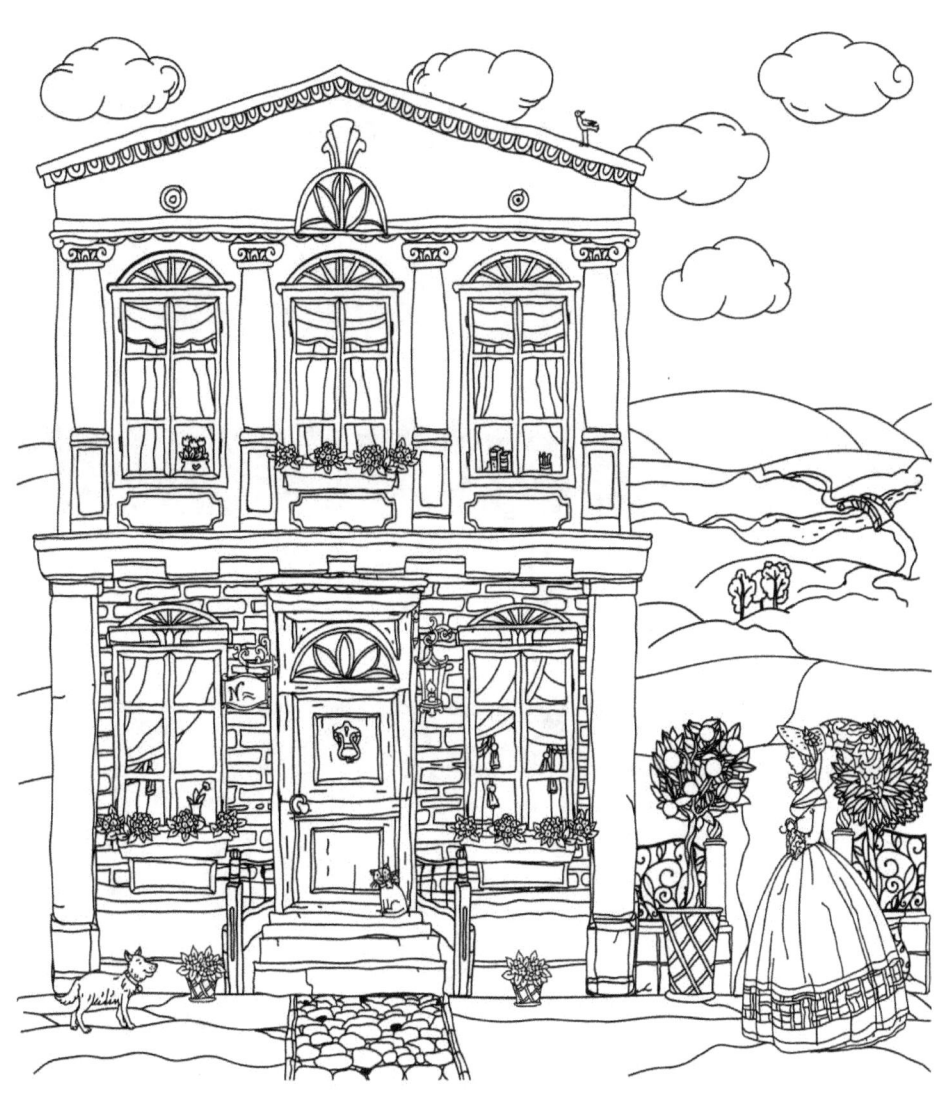

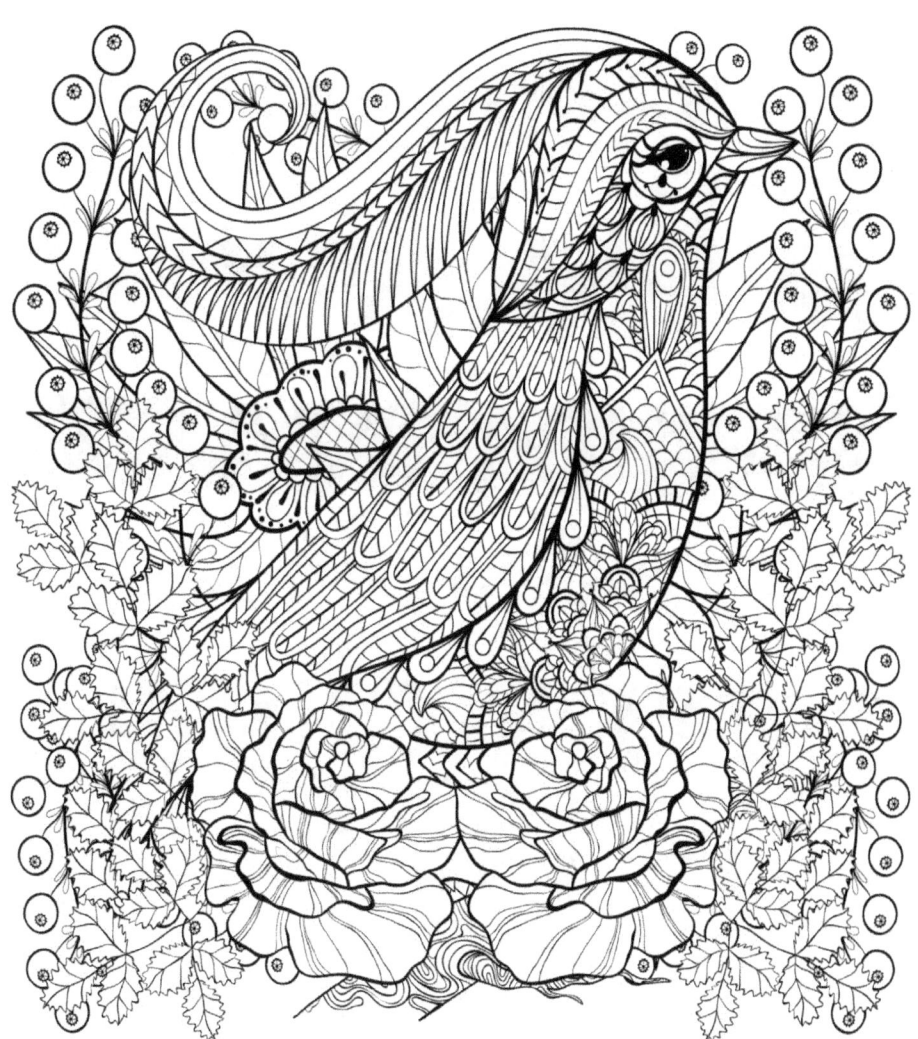

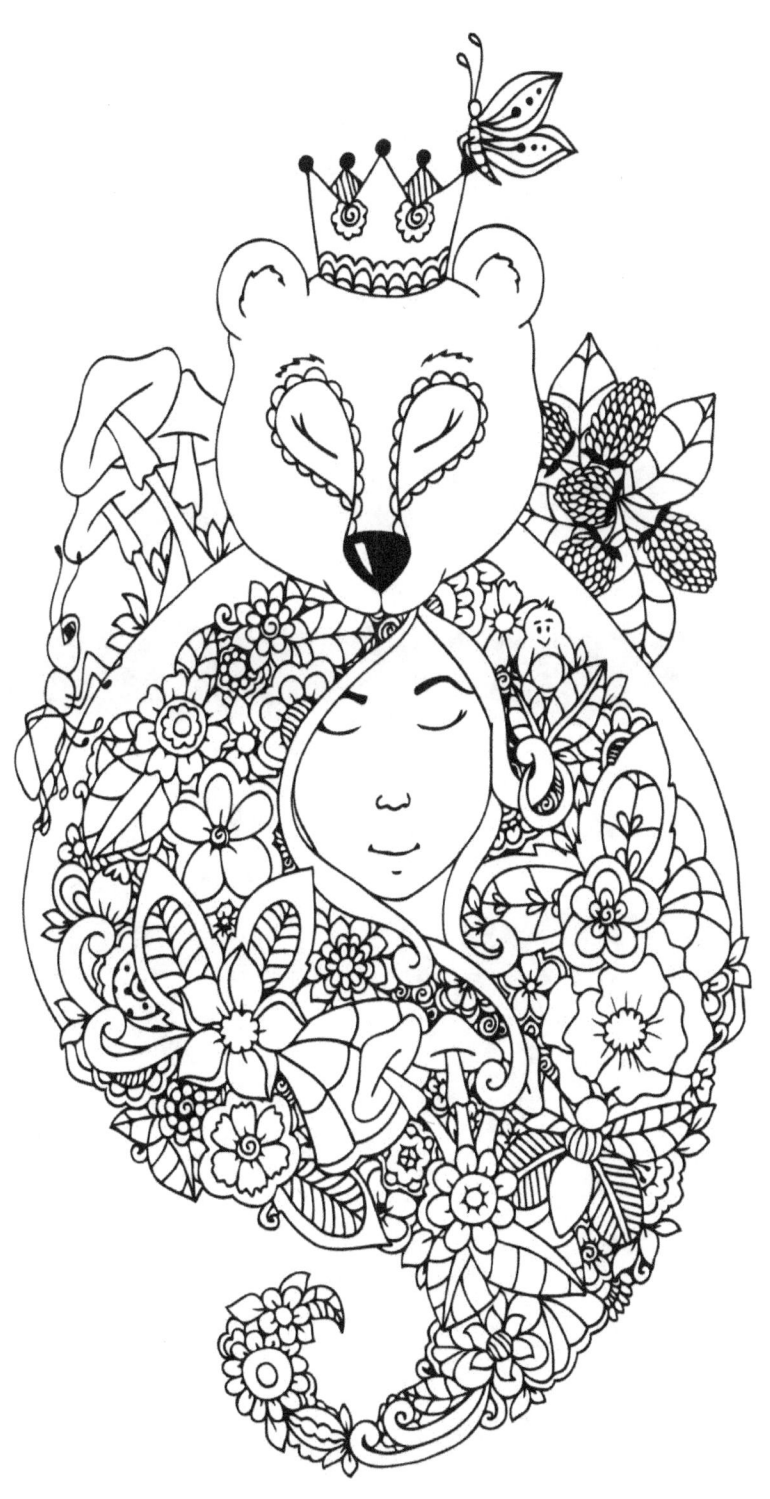

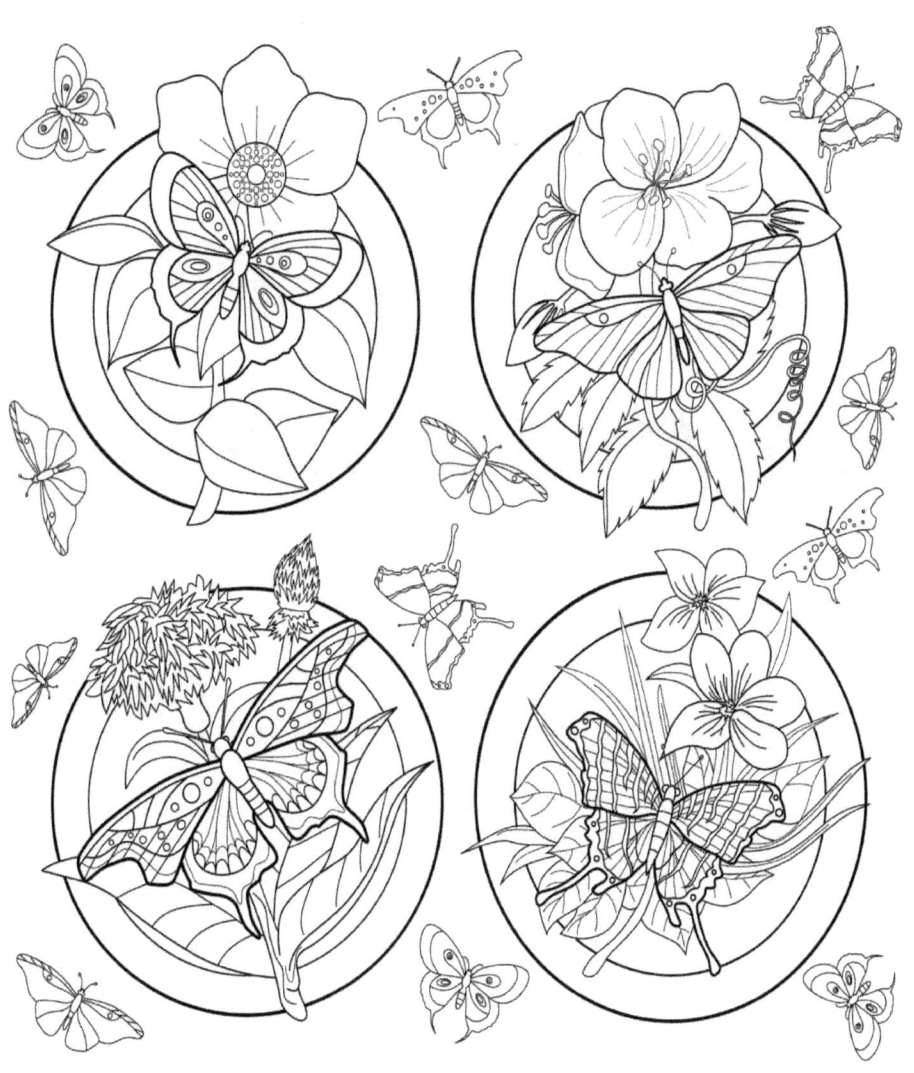

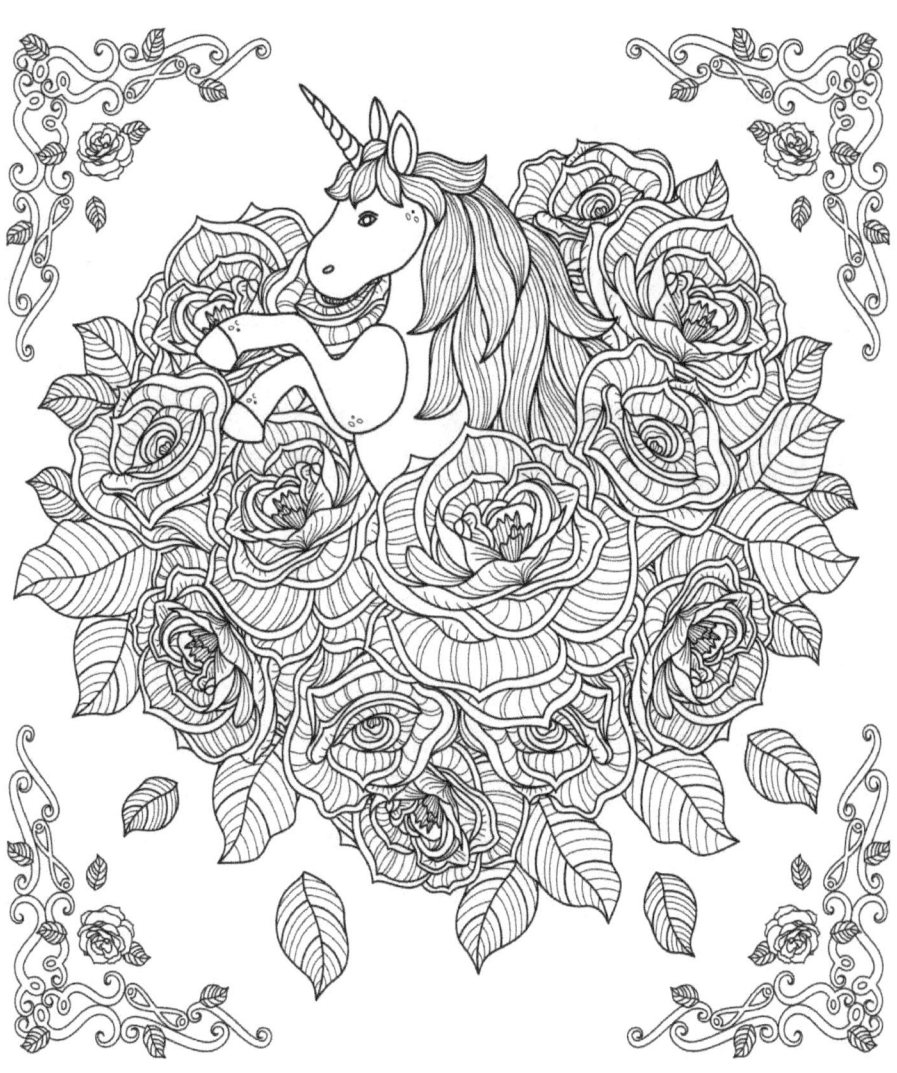

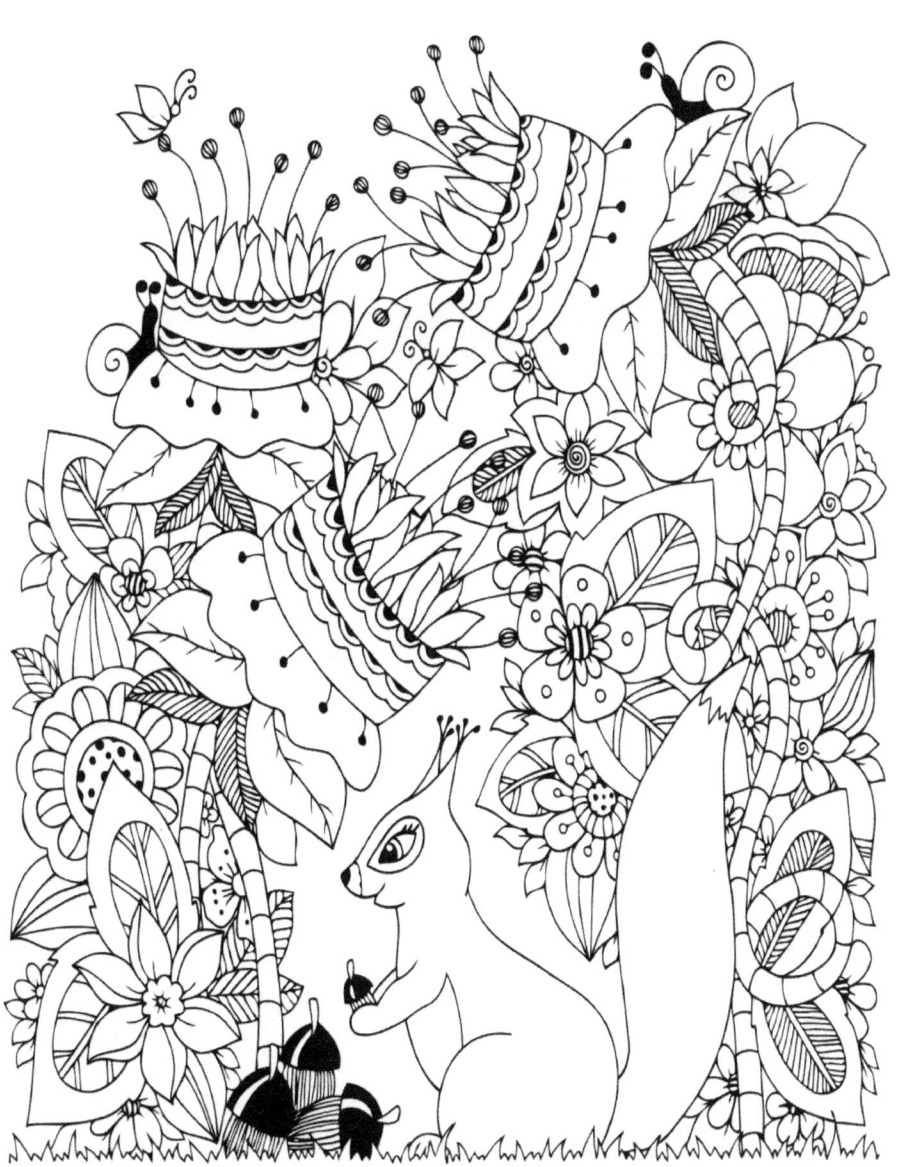

www.ingramcontent.com/pod-product-compliance
Lightning Source LLC
Chambersburg PA
CBHW070134210526
45170CB00013B/1009